GALVESTON, SOUTH PADRE ISLAND & THE TEXAS GULF COAST

GALVESTON, SOUTH PADRE ISLAND & THE TEXAS GULF COAST

Includes Corpus Christi

Alex Wukman

The Countryman Press
Woodstock, Vermont

DEDICATION

To those who believed I say thank you
To those who doubted I say I told you
To those who dream I say I am you

ISBN 978-1-58157-039-7

Cover photo © Zaque Pollard/SPICVB
Interior photos by the author unless otherwise specified
Book design Bodenweber Design
Page composition by S.E. Livingston
Maps by Mapping Specialists, Ltd., Madison, WI, © The Countryman Press

Published by The Countryman Press, P.O. Box 748, Woodstock, Vermont 05091

Distributed by W. W. Norton & Company, Inc., 500 Fifth Ave., New York, NY 10110

Printed in the United States of America

10 9 8 7 6 5 4 3 2 1

GREAT DESTINATIONS TRAVEL GUIDEBOOK SERIES

Recommended by *National Geographic Traveler* and *Travel + Leisure* magazines.

[A] CRISP AND CRITICAL APPROACH, FOR TRAVELERS WHO WANT TO LIVE LIKE LOCALS.
—*USA Today*

Great Destinations™ guidebooks are known for their comprehensive, critical coverage of regions of extraordinary cultural interest and natural beauty. The authors in this series are professional travel writers who have lived for many years in the regions they describe. Each title in this series is continuously updated with each printing to insure accurate and timely information. All the books contain more than one hundred photographs and maps.

Current titles available:

THE ADIRONDACK BOOK
ATLANTA
AUSTIN, SAN ANTONIO & THE TEXAS HILL COUNTRY
THE BERKSHIRE BOOK
BIG SUR, MONTEREY BAY & GOLD COAST WINE COUNTRY
CAPE CANAVERAL, COCOA BEACH & FLORIDA'S SPACE COAST
THE CHARLESTON, SAVANNAH & COASTAL ISLANDS BOOK
THE CHESAPEAKE BAY BOOK
THE COAST OF MAINE BOOK
COLORADO'S CLASSIC MOUNTAIN TOWNS: GREAT DESTINATIONS
THE FINGER LAKES BOOK
GALVESTON, SOUTH PADRE ISLAND & THE TEXAS GULF COAST
THE HAMPTONS BOOK
HONOLULU & OAHU: GREAT DESTINATIONS HAWAII
THE HUDSON VALLEY BOOK
LOS CABOS & BAJA CALIFORNIA SUR: GREAT DESTINATIONS MEXICO
THE NANTUCKET BOOK
THE NAPA & SONOMA BOOK
PALM BEACH, MIAMI & THE FLORIDA KEYS
PHOENIX, SCOTTSDALE, SEDONA & CENTRAL ARIZONA
PLAYA DEL CARMEN, TULUM & THE RIVIERA MAYA: GREAT DESTINATIONS MEXICO
SALT LAKE CITY, PARK CITY, PROVO & UTAH'S HIGH COUNTRY RESORTS
SAN DIEGO & TIJUANA
SAN JUAN, VIEQUES & CULEBRA: GREAT DESTINATIONS PUERTO RICO
THE SANTA FE & TAOS BOOK
THE SARASOTA, SANIBEL ISLAND & NAPLES BOOK
THE SEATTLE & VANCOUVER BOOK: INCLUDES THE OLYMPIC PENINSULA, VICTORIA & MORE
THE SHENANDOAH VALLEY BOOK
TOURING EAST COAST WINE COUNTRY

If you are traveling to, moving to, residing in, or just interested in any (or all!) of these enchanting regions, a Great Destinations guidebook is a superior companion. Honest and painstakingly critical, full of information only a local can provide, Great Destinations guidebooks give you all the practical knowledge you need to enjoy the best of each region. Why not own them all?

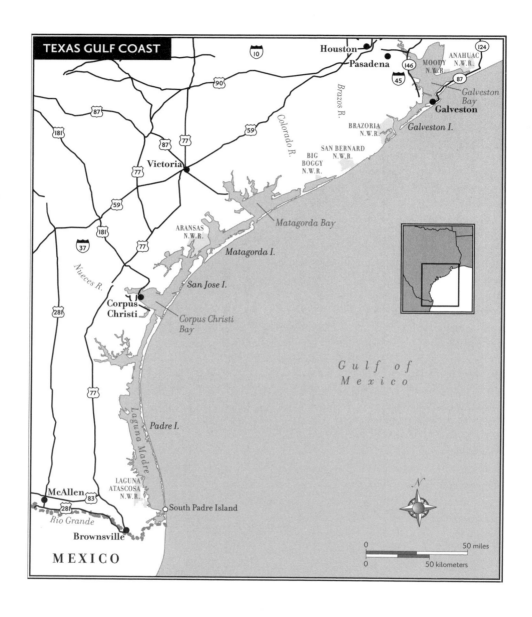

TEXAS GULF COAST

Houston
Pasadena
ANAHUAC
N.W.R.
MOODY
N.W.R.
Galveston
Bay
Galveston
Galveston I.
BRAZORIA
N.W.R.
SAN BERNARD
N.W.R.
BIG
BOGGY
N.W.R.
Brazos R.
Colorado R.
Victoria
Matagorda Bay
ARANSAS
N.W.R.
Matagorda I.
San Jose I.
Corpus
Christi
Corpus Christi
Bay
Nueces R.
Gulf of
Mexico
Padre I.
Laguna Madre
LAGUNA
ATASCOSA
N.W.R.
McAllen
South Padre Island
Rio Grande
Brownsville
MEXICO

N

0   50 miles
0   50 kilometers

CONTENTS

Acknowledgments

I owe a huge debt of gratitude to more people than I can name for helping me through the extremely difficult process of this book. I owe a world of apology to everyone I blew off while I was working on it, and a beer to half of Montrose. If I listed everyone who helped with advice, knowledge, or just by being in the right place at the right time, I would never be finished. So I'll keep it short.

My family for their peculiar way of showing love.

My friends for their understanding.

And above all Kim Grant, my editor, for doing the one thing no one else would do: give me a chance.

Introduction

The driving distance between Galveston Island and South Padre Island is about 400 miles, roughly the same distance as from New York City to the North Carolina state line. The drive can take anywhere from 7 to 10 hours, depending on speed and stops. There are dozens of hamlets and fishing villages, a handful of cities, three international airports, and a whole lot of nothing on that drive. It's completely possible to go for hours without seeing another car, and for miles with only the birds, sun, and cows to testify you were there.

This vast emptiness exists despite the fact that the urban and suburban centers of the Texas coast are some of the fastest-growing areas in the nation. Some analysts predict that the area will keep growing with a 10 percent increase in multinational transplants every year. It is not uncommon to run into an Austrian buying gas in Houston, an Englishman at a bar in Galveston, or a German sitting down for dinner in Corpus Christi.

The population of full-time residents for South Padre Island, the main resort destination of the state, has doubled within the last 15 years, and the population of coastal cities like the Houston-Galveston metropolitan area is expected to double within 10 years.

The main reason for this increasing population growth is energy. Texas is a key hub in the oil and natural gas chain; this means that household names like ChevronTexaco, ExxonMobil, DuPont, and BP have corporate offices in Houston and refineries in Pasadena, Texas City, Angleton, and Freeport.

Yet the stretch of beaches from Galveston to South Padre is one of the most underdeveloped in the country. Part of this is because the Texas coast is home to 20 different state and national parks. This reverence for wildlife and wide-open spaces, combined with most towns being little more than fishing villages and the presence of large oil companies, makes for an interesting experience. It can best be summed up as driving past 45 minutes of a Dow Chemical plant that sits on the border of a national wildlife refuge to arrive at a point on the map where there is little more than a bait camp.

It's a common occurrence to see supertankers, shrimp boats, and jack-up rigs passing one another in the canals and channels while local men and women stand on the jetty to catch flounder and redfish at three in the morning, guided only by the lights strung from their portable generators. It almost goes without saying that the people of the Texas coast are a breed unto themselves, fiercely loyal, fiercely private, and fiercely independent. Their lives are still bound to the land and the water in ways that haven't substantially changed in a hundred years. Many never leave the towns they were born in. Their history of the area is personal. Personal tragedies and comedies mark every rock, sand dune, and shoal. Sitting in a bar, bait camp, living

A garden sundial.

room, or porch swing, residents will reel off story after story, some with names and dates that go back to the days before the first cars made their appearances south of the Brazos River.

Then, of course, there is the collective history of neighbors, the stories that make a place unique and special to all those that live there. The stories that come from the bygone days when life was rougher and simpler, the ones that often get left out of the history books they use down at the high school.

On the Texas coast those stories are often written in blood and iron. From the tales brought back by Cabeza de Vaca of cannibal Indians, through the revolutionary slaughter at San Jacinto, up to World War II when a Nazi U-boat was sighted in Galveston harbor, real estate on the Texas coast has been bought with the lives of soldiers and civilians.

Sometimes that bloodshed was righteous and just, such as when Rafael

The Bolivar Point Lighthouse is one of the few lighthouses on the Texas coast still standing.

Rescindez-Ramirez, "The Railway Killer," was captured after murdering dozens of women throughout the country. Other times the bloodshed was political, like when the U.S. and Mexico disputed the territory between the Nueces and Rio Grande Rivers—including present day Corpus Christi, Brownsville, and South Padre—and that dispute led to the Mexican-American war. The deaths haven't always been clean or honorable, as was the case when the Mexican Army slaughtered the garrison at Goliad; but the spilled blood has always watered the tree of peace.

This history of violence begetting peace helps explain why the modern Texas coast is a remarkably low-crime area. Despite the fact that illegal immigration and drug smuggling are daily realities here, life has an almost prosaic feel at times. Part of that laid-back attitude can perhaps best be summed up in an overheard comment at one of the local high school graduations: "Baby, it's too hot to be pretentious." And it's almost too hot to be passionate about a cause; on a 90-degrees-in-the-shade summer day, it's hard to imagine people fighting for the sand that blows across the parking lot of the 7-Eleven or dying for the surf that crashes outside the hotel room window in the glow of the setting sun.

Children bobbing and playing in the waves breaking on the shore, a surfer pulling a hard right at the second sandbar, while a mile or so out a fishing boat cruises toward what the captain thinks is a slick of speckled trout—these are the realities of the Texas coast, not the worlds-away-worries of the border or the hear-about-it-on-the-nightly-news horrors of the city. People don't come to the beach to worry; they come to relax.

The Way This Book Works

Criteria for Inclusion

As I researched and wrote this book I was guided by one main goal: to try to change the opinion many people have of the Texas coast and the people who live there. I wanted to show that there is more to do than fish, hunt, and play bingo. I wanted to help people to understand that the coast isn't all oil refineries, power plants, and bait camps. In some ways I feel I succeeded, in others I feel I failed. This bittersweet sensation is primarily because I worry I may have been too selective. As I was writing this book I found myself omitting many scenic places, towns that are rich in local character, in order to focus more on the towns that featured cultural high points. I may have neglected a fishing spot when I could instead mention a ballet, or a particularly good hunting area when I could talk about a symphony. I also may not have had room for towns that had a roadside attraction as their main claim to fame. When choosing between, say, an alligator farm and a good but little-known restaurant, I usually felt I had to go with the side of sophistication. Now that I've said that, I have to fess up: I didn't include all the cultural highlights or areas of sophistication on the Texas Gulf Coast. I left out Houston. I know the criticism; I've already heard the arguments. And my response is fairly simple: I left out Houston for specific reasons, not the least of which is that Houston is not on the coast—it is 35 miles inland. The Army Corps of Engineers brought the coast *to* Houston. The second reason is that Houston is far too big and far too complex to be a simple chapter; it requires its own book. The third is that Houston casts such a giant shadow over Texas, both by its size and by its notoriety, that it obscures many of the other cities in the state, and I felt it was time to give some of the smaller places on the coast their due.

Methods of Payment

Throughout this book you will see listings for what types of credit cards an establishment accepts, but not for whether it accepts checks. The main reason for this is that very few establishments on the Texas coast accept checks anymore. Most hotels and rental car companies do, but outside that it's a gamble. Some stores do, but many don't. Most bars and nightclubs don't. Blame it on the fact that Texas has one of the highest incidences of theft by check in the United States. Therefore, if you are planning on using checks during your trip, it is best to call ahead to see which establishments accept them and what their particular policy is regarding them. Throughout the book, major credit card companies are indicated by their initials. The abbreviations are as follows:

AE: American Express	CB: Carte Blanche
D: Discover	DC: Diner's Club
MC: MasterCard	V: Visa

Some places may accept others, like the Japanese Credit Bureau card, but since they make up such a small minority I avoided mentioning them. If you plan on using such a card, please call ahead to find out if it is accepted.

Prices

There is an old newspaper saw about discussing prices in print: "Writing about how much things cost is like waltzing to the weather report—it can be done, but the outcome won't be very pretty." To make the point a little clearer, because of the considerable discrepancy in the socioeconomic circumstances of people visiting the Texas coast, there is no right way to discuss, let alone write about, price. Here's a for instance: To some, spending $100 night on a hotel is a steal, to others it's a normal trip expense, to still others it takes a large bite out of their budget, while to some it's an impossible dream. I bring this up to show the arbitrary aspects of the rating system I used. It's broken down like this:

	Restaurant	*Lodging*
Inexpensive	under $25	under $75
Moderate	$25 to $50	$75 to $100
Expensive	$50 to $75	$100 to $150
Very Expensive	$75 and up	$150 and up

This is all based on paying for two people. The room rate for lodging is based on a two-person, single-night stay in the peak months, and the restaurant prices are based on appetizer/side dish, main course, and nonalcoholic drinks for two. Drinks, taxes, and tips are all extras. I also should mention that in sections labeled "vacation rentals," no price or payment information is listed, because so many variables are involved. For example, discounts are given based on the length of stay, time of year, and even the attitude of the rental agent.

Texas Roadway Peculiarities

An intersection in downtown Freeport, Texas.

Texas more than almost any other state has embraced the highway; it probably has something to do with all those wide-open spaces. This love affair between Texas and the freeway goes so deep that Texas towns name them. It may sound silly until you want to get to the airport and someone tells you to take the Gulf Freeway, someone else tells you to take the North Freeway, and a third tells you to take I-45, and you finally realize they are all talking about the same freeway. I know it doesn't make any sense, but you have to understand that many things don't make a lot of sense in Texas, especially when it comes to the roads. They differ so much from city to city that it is almost impossible to make a clear general assessment. The best that can be done is to try to explain the most common and confusing terms. The first is "feeder road." A feeder road or, as it is also known, a frontage road, is a road that runs beside a highway and allows cars to enter and exit fairly easily and businesses to draw a freeway address. These are common in Texas, as are "FM" designations. FM is a Texas Department of Transportation abbreviation that simply means Farm to Market and is used to distinguish these roads from state highways, U.S. highways, and interstates.

Drinking and Driving

This is one of the most serious subjects in Texas, so serious in fact that the U.S. Navy makes special mention of it for sailors and pilots assigned to Naval Air Station Corpus Christi. In Texas a first offense for driving while intoxicated (DWI) can result in the loss of your driver's license, a $2,000 fine, and two years in jail. You really don't want to know what happens on the second. If you are driving, you are viewed by the law as consenting to a Breathalyzer test; refusal to take one can cost you your license. In fact, no one in a motor vehicle, not just the driver, is allowed to have an open container of alcohol. This has been interpreted to mean any alcoholic container with a broken seal. Having an open container of alcohol is probable cause for a DWI. Having an empty alcohol container is probable cause for a DWI. Even if you are in your parked car and the keys are in the ignition, you can get a DWI; the keys imply that you will be driving. It should also be noted that police checkpoints are common in some Texas cities and that cab drivers have been known to take people who pass out in their cabs to police stations.

Seafood

There is an old saying on the Gulf Coast (and elsewhere), never to eat oysters in months without an "r." This is because eating raw oysters in the summer can lead to contracting one of eight different food-borne illnesses, including hepatitis A and salmonella. All it takes to reduce the potential of getting infected is to cook the oysters. However, not all problems with seafood can be solved simply by cooking it. There are some species that have to be avoided. The main one is speckled trout, also known as spotted sea trout. The reason for this is the high concentration of PCBs (polychlorinated biphenyls) in their fatty tissue. PCBs do a wide range of damage to people who inadvertently consume them. For pregnant women the possible effects include lowered birth weights, which can delay phys- ical development in children and create learning difficulties. For adults PCBs have been known to damage the immune system, reproductive organs, skin, stomach, thyroid, kid- neys and liver. They also may increase the risk of cancer. Diners should also avoid catfish and blue crabs taken from Galveston Bay. This is because of a high presence of dioxins in them. Most bay seafood sold on the Texas coast comes from the lesser polluted Vermillion Bay in Louisiana.

Events

Throughout this book I have avoided listing locations for some events because of the fact that certain seasonal events are prone to move, and in some cases (say Mardi Gras or spring break) the dates can change considerably from year to year. Which is why in many cases I listed the time of the month that the event occurs. If you are planning your trip

Galveston shrimp boats ply the waters of the Gulf, ensuring that only the freshest shrimp make it to the table.

around a specific event or a series of events, please contact the specific town or city's chamber of commerce or convention and visitors bureau for more up-to-date information. All the necessary visitor contact information for each of the main three cities in this book—Galveston, Corpus Christi, and South Padre Island—has been listed in the back of the book under the heading of Information.

National and State Parks

The Texas coast is well-covered with 30 national and state parks. They vary in size from the relatively modest and sparse San Jacinto Battleground and Monument, which is a mere 1,200 acres, to the massive Padre Island National Seashore, which runs the length of three counties. The amount of parks in this part of the state, combined with the Texas Open Beaches Act (which states that all land from the water to the vegetation line is public property), has helped to keep the amount of development minimal, the majority of beaches fairly protected, and the population on the coast small. I probably should take a moment to explain just how isolated some of these parks are. The best way to describe it is to quote an old Texas coastal maxim: "You're either exactly where you want to be or lost." Most of these parks aren't like Yellowstone. In fact, some of the island parks have no bridges connecting them to the mainland, while a few of the mainland parks have no roads. The only way to get around in some parks is in a shallow-draft boat. And at one park, the only structure is a helipad that Chevron uses to evacuate its people from offshore oil rigs in case of a hurricane. If you want to go camping at any of the parks, you should talk to the Texas State Parks and Wildlife Department or the U.S. Parks Department to determine what accommodations are available, because at some of these parks the only things you will have are what you bring in. It is worth mentioning that no fishing license is required to fish from the shore or a pier in a state park; however, if you fish from a boat you need a license. All state-mandated size and bag limits apply.

It also is worth mentioning that with an Annual Public Hunting Permit, which costs $48, it is perfectly legal to kill game-species animals in specific state parks. If you win the random drawing, you even get a guided hunt. For more information on this, visit the Texas Parks and Wildlife Division Web site, www.tpwd.state.tx.us. You can even hunt on National Wildlife Refuges, which are described by the U.S. Fish and Wildlife Service as "the only national system of lands dedicated to conserving our wildlife heritage for today and generations yet to come." Of course, nonhunters, in planning their visits, should take care to determine when and where hunting is permitted.

Please remember the parks listed here are only a sampling of the many state and national parks on the Texas coast. A quick note: If you are planning on camping outdoors overnight in Texas, you should probably limit your travels to the Gulf Coast to March, April, October, and November. This is because summers are hot and humid, and the nights are filled with mosquitoes. Winters are cold and wet, with temperatures that can drop 20 degrees in an hour.

Parks on the Texas Coast

ANAHUAC NATIONAL WILDLIFE REFUGE
409-267-3337
www.fws.gov/refuges
509 Washington Ave., Anahuac, TX 77514

This 34,000-acre refuge was established in 1963 and is part of the 540 parks that make up the National Wildlife Refuge System. October through March, when the waterfowl migrate, are the prime months for Anahuac. Twenty-seven species of ducks and as many as 80,000 geese regularly winter here. This of course draws hunters; 40 percent of the refuge is open to duck and goose hunters. Three different hunt units provide access to hunt areas by foot or by boat. For disabled hunters there is an easily accessible blind—provided on a first-come, first-served basis.

ARANSAS NATIONAL WILDLIFE REFUGE
361-286-3559
www.fws.gov/refuges
1 Wildlife Circle, Austwell, TX 77950

This refuge was established by FDR in 1937 and has come to be known as the winter home to the largest flock of endangered whooping cranes in the world. It also has a 40- foot observation tower and a winding boardwalk that provide beautiful views of San Antonio Bay and the Intracoastal Waterway.

SAN JACINTO BATTLEGROUND / MONUMENT & BATTLESHIP TEXAS
281-479-2431
www.tpwd.state.tx.us
3523 Hwy. 134, La Porte TX 77571

When the battleship *Texas* was decommissioned in 1948, it became the first battleship memorial museum in the nation. The ship was later presented to the state of Texas and recommissioned as the flagship of the Texas Navy. It is permanently anchored on Buffalo Bayou and the Houston Ship Channel at the San Jacinto Battleground Historic Site. As almost every Texas schoolchild knows, the San Jacinto battleground is where Sam Houston's forces routed General Santa Anna's army and won Texas its independence from Mexico.

FULTON MANSION STATE HISTORIC SITE
361-729-0386
www.tpwd.state.tx.us
317 N. Fulton Beach Rd., Rockport, TX 78382

Built in 1877, this luxurious house featured all the modern conveniences of the Victorian era, including indoor plumbing, central heat, and gas lights. It also is a prime example of high-Victorian architecture. For the true historic-home buff, this is not to be missed.

GALVESTON ISLAND STATE PARK
409-737-1222
www.tpwd.state.tx.us
14901 FM 3005, Galveston, TX 77554

This 2,013-acre park is located on the western end of Galveston Island. It offers camping, birding, bike riding, fishing, swimming, and summer plays at the Mary Moody Northern Amphitheater. It also is part of the Dunes Renewal Project. In September 1998 Tropical

Egrets are common sights on the Texas coast.

Storm Frances destroyed the sand dunes, which are the only protection for the park's facilities. In an inspired attempt to rebuild the dunes, the Texas Parks and Wildlife Department asked residents to bring down their Christmas trees to be placed on the beach; ten years later the program is working fairly well.

GOOSE ISLAND STATE PARK

361-729-2858
www.tpwd.state.tx.us
202 S. Palmetto St., Rockport, TX

Developed by the Civilian Conservation Corps in the early 1930s, this park is fairly sparse. It has no swimming area, even though it's on Aransas Bay. This is because the main coastal area is composed of a concrete bulkhead, oyster shells, a mud flat, and marsh grass. So the three things to do here are camp, watch birds, and fish—in fact the park will loan you fishing tackle. The park also allows motorized boats. The only facilities include shade shelter campsites (they are known as open cabanas), which have water and electricity. They are located throughout the park. The best time to come to this park is in the winter, since it is directly across St. Charles Bay from the wintering grounds of whooping cranes.

LAGUNA ATASCOSA NATIONAL WILDLIFE REFUGE

956-748-3607
www.fws.gov/refuges
P.O. Box 450, Rio Hondo, TX 78583

This small out-of-the-way spot is a bird watcher's dream. Over 400 different species have been sighted here. One of the truly spectacular things about this park is that more than 80 percent of the North American population of redhead ducks winters here. It also is home to populations of ocelot and jaguarundi—two endangered species of big cat. The volunteers and staff combined their efforts to build a butterfly garden, which attracts examples of over half the butterfly species found in the United States, plus rare Mexican species. One of the more incredible things to see is the nesting of the Kemp's ridley sea turtles, when they come to shore, lay their eggs, and swim back out to sea.

MATAGORDA ISLAND WILDLIFE MANAGEMENT AREA
979-244-6804
www.tpwd.state.tx.us
1700 Seventh St., Bay City, TX 77414

This is one of the state parks that excels at being primitive. There are no supplies here but what you bring in, catch, kill, or find. No electricity, running water, shelter, or food. No motorized vehicles are allowed on the interior of the island. The activities that are allowed are deer hunting (in season), fishing, birding, and picnicking. The main scenic point here is the lighthouse, which dates to 1852. There are alligators here, so be careful.

PADRE ISLAND NATIONAL SEASHORE
361-949-8068
www.nps.gov/pais
20402 Park Road 22, Corpus Christi, TX 78418

This 130,434-acre stretch of barrier island was established as a park on September 28, 1962. It is one of the only parks in Texas to be managed by the National Park Service. Among its unique features: Starting in 2001, the government began to allow drilling for oil and gas here. It is also one of the few parks that allows 24-hour, year-round access.

PORT ISABEL LIGHTHOUSE STATE HISTORIC SITE
956-943-2262
www.tpwd.state.tx.us
421 E. Queen Isabel Blvd., Port Isabel, TX 78578

The lamp in this 72-foot lighthouse was lit in 1852. It burned through the Union blockade, the battle of Palmito Ranch in 1865, and the Mexican War battles of Palo Alto and Resaca de la Palma. It withstood hurricanes, floods, and fires. But it couldn't withstand technology and politics. A few years after this lighthouse opened it was obsolete—newer, taller, more powerful lighthouses opened. Then the railroads came to South Texas. They linked Corpus to the interior of Mexico and the rest of the United States. This, more than anything, stopped the ships from coming. Then depression hit. The 1890s were awful for this part of the nation—the banks were failing, the prices of crops dropped, and unemployment soared. While things improved for the country, they didn't for the lighthouse. Finally in 1905 the staff stopped hoping times were going to get better and turned off the light for good. For 42 years the lighthouse stood neglected, until the state park board approved funds for the restoration. It took five years of hard work before the state dedicated the lighthouse as a landmark in 1952 and another 50 for it to be fully restored to its circa-1880 prime.

One of the festive arches that play a large role in Galveston's Mardi Gras celebration.

GALVESTON

Grand Old Lady of the Gulf

For thousands of years the site of Galveston has been inhabited by humans. Centuries before the first Europeans came to North America, *Auia*, as Galveston was then known, served as the summer fishing grounds for various Indian tribes, including Akokisas, Lipan Apaches, and Karankawas. Although Galveston Island was discovered in 1519 by Juan de Grijalva, a Spanish explorer, it was not until 1528, when Álvar Núñez Cabeza de Vaca and 15 of his men shipwrecked on what he would later call the Island of Doom—which may well have been Galveston Island, although some historians remain unsure—that Europeans would set foot near here.

During the years Cabeza de Vaca was stranded on the coast, he and his shipmates were reduced to cannibalism, revered as shamans, and treated as slaves. After Cabeza de Vaca and the surviving members of his party made their escape, it would be almost a century and a half before another European would come to the region. In 1684 René Robert Cavalier, Sieur de La Salle, left France with 300 colonists, planning to found a settlement near the mouth of the Mississippi. Instead, after a disastrous voyage, he was stranded in February 1685 with his remaining followers near Matagorda Bay, to the southwest. He claimed the region for France. His tenure on the Gulf Coast would be just as unfortunate—he was killed by his own men as he led an expedition eastward to find the Mississippi River.

One hundred years later the Spanish colonial governor Bernardo de Gálvez sent José de Evia to chart the Gulf of Mexico from the Texas coast to New Orleans. On July 23, 1786, Evia charted an area near the mouth of a river and named the island he saw Isla de San Luis and the eastern tip of it "Pt. de Culebras"—Snake Point. He named the bay after Gálvez, and the island and the city that grew on it later took the name Galveston. However, Gálvez died before he could set foot on his namesake.

A PIRATE HAVEN

In 1816 French privateer Louis Michel Aury arrived with 13 ships and established a base. He was quickly joined by Francisco Xavier Mina, who soon departed to invade Mexico. By the time Jean Laffite arrived on the island in 1817 there were approximately a thousand residents. Laffite was appointed governor of Galveston by the embryonic Republic of Mexico. Laffite established his own fortified settlement, named it Campeche, and made it his home base. The fort he built was destroyed in 1818 by one of Galveston's infamous storms. By the following year the little village Laffite constructed contained huts for the

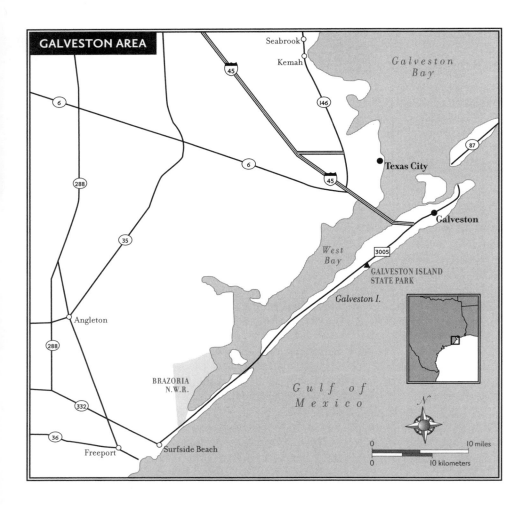

pirates, a large and illegal slave market, boardinghouses for slave merchants and buyers, a shipyard, saloons, and Laffite's own house, the Maison Rouge. At its peak Campeche may have been home to between a thousand and two thousand people. Laffite was also "appointed" governor by James Long, a filibustering American merchant who was attempting to drive the Spanish royalists from Texas and establish a republican government. Long established his own headquarters at Bolivar Point, Fort Las Casas, in September 1819. In 1821 Long led an expedition to invade Mexico and capture La Bahia. (He himself was eventually captured, freed when Mexico finally achieved its independence from Spain, then died in Mexico City under mysterious circumstances.)

In May of 1821, after Long had left for Mexico, Laffite had attacked an American ship, an action that forced him to abandon his Galveston base. Before leaving he treated his followers and crew to a gala celebration complete with wine, women, and whiskey. At the

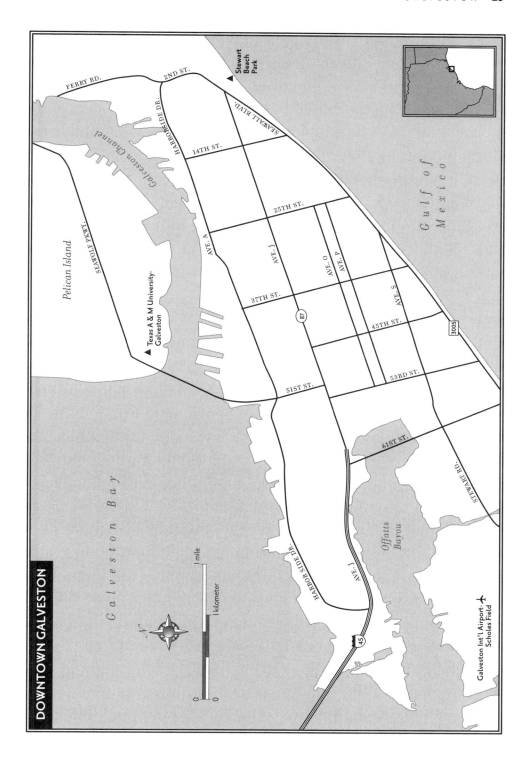

DOWNTOWN GALVESTON

Gulf of Mexico

Galveston Bay

Pelican Island

Galveston Channel

Stewart Beach Park

FERRY RD.

2ND ST.

HARBORSIDE DR.

SEAWALL BLVD.

14TH ST.

25TH ST.

37TH ST.

45TH ST.

51ST ST.

53RD ST.

61ST ST.

AVE. A

AVE. J

AVE. O

AVE. P

AVE. S

AVE. J

AVE. J

SEAWOLF PKWY.

HARBOR SIDE DR.

STEWART RD.

Offatts Bayou

Texas A & M University-Galveston

Galveston Int'l Airport-Scholes Field

87

3005

45

N

1 mile

1 kilometer

0

0

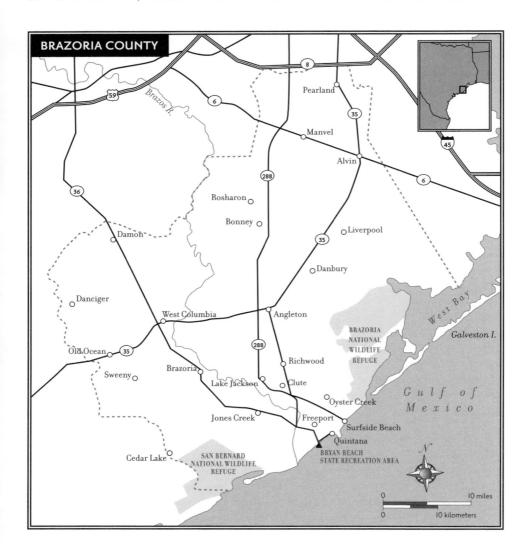

evening's climax Laffite set fire to his own house and then the entire town of Campeche. It is rumored that before abandoning Galveston, Laffite buried treasure throughout the island, although none has ever been found. It is also rumored that Laffite fled to Mexico, faked his own death, and returned to Galveston under the assumed name Meazall, which his descendants still carry.

TEXAS DECLARES INDEPENDENCE

In 1830 the Mexican government sent John Davis Bradburn to establish a garrison on the northeastern edge of Galveston Bay at Anahuac. This move angered the residents and prompted the Anahuac disturbances. This led to the arrest of many Galveston Bay residents. When Texas declared its independence from Mexico in 1836, the Texas Navy headquartered four of its ships on the island. The primary mission of these ships was to prevent the Mexican Navy from resupplying General Santa Anna's troops, something that assisted in Santa Anna's defeat at the Battle of San Jacinto 22 miles to the northwest.

> The method of transmission for yellow fever was identified in 1900 by Dr. Walter Reed, who also proposed ways to combat and control the spread of the disease. His suggestions were put to the test in 1905 when a yellow fever epidemic broke out in New Orleans. His methods proved so successful that the 1905 epidemic was the last in the United States. (*From the U.S. Centers for Disease Control.*)

On the heels of Texas independence, Canadian entrepreneur Michael B. Menard purchased a "league and labor" of land from the Republic of Texas, on which he established the city of Galveston, with an area of seven square miles. In order to promote his fledgling town, Menard formed the Galveston City Company with nine other prominent Texans. Among them was Gail Borden Jr., the inventor of condensed milk. Some of the first actions undertaken by Menard and his associates were the construction of a post office and naval base on the island, two firsts of their kind for Texas. In 1837 the Texas Congress designated Galveston as a "port of entry" and named Borden as the collector of customs. Two years later Galveston suffered its first yellow fever epidemic. Over the next 30 years, such outbreaks would become almost a regular occurrence in Galveston history. These horrific epidemics were caused by the influx of new, more virulent strains of disease from the increased steamer traffic, introduced to a rapidly growing population in a city with poor waste management and even worse drainage—ideal for the disease-carrying mosquitoes.

When Texas was admitted into the Union in 1845, Galveston was the largest city in the new state, with a population of 3,500 and a booming economy. The editor of the *Galveston Daily News* estimated in 1858 that the economy was growing at 50 percent a year, despite the fact that the city had no manufacturing base. However, all was not perfect, as over the horizon loomed the gathering clouds of civil war. Secession was not a particularly popular idea in Galveston during 1860, owing to the city's rapidly growing merchant class and large immigrant population, many of whom were German; by this time the city numbered near seven thousand residents, and a causeway had been completed to the mainland. Nevertheless, in February 1861, before Lincoln's inauguration, Texas did secede from the Union, and with the overwhelming support of Galveston voters. Galveston's German émigrés were almost completely pro-Union and very unhappy. Secession was even less popular with the merchants—a majority of whom were slaveholding members of the Whig party—primarily because they had extensive commercial ties to the great eastern cities of New York, Boston, and Philadelphia, as well as to London and Paris. They feared that any disruption to the Union would inevitably lead to a disruption in their business. Sadly, they were right.

BLOCKADE AND CIVIL WAR

In June of 1861 President Lincoln ordered a blockade of the Gulf Coast. Secession and the blockade order had a profound impact on Galveston's economy, so much so that by the time the USS *South Carolina* dropped anchor in Galveston harbor in July, shortages were already being felt and unemployment was on the rise. After her arrival, the *South Carolina*, a screw-driven steamer, made some quick captures of overzealous sailing vessels trying to break through the newly erected blockade. It is reported that she nabbed 11 vessels in the first five days of the blockade. (Later, blockade-runners would be much better prepared and prove more elusive.)

This sent the Galveston economy into a tailspin. Shops were left unable to meet payroll, and the majority of them had to close. When word reached the Confederate military's high command that Galveston had been blockaded, they were torn—some felt that Galveston was excessively vulnerable to invasion and not worth the effort to defend; others saw it as having symbolic value.

The romantics won, and preparations against an anticipated invasion began. Two small forts were built to defend the island, one on the Bolivar Peninsula, the other at Pelican Spit, and an observation post was built on the Hendley building. By August tension and boredom had started to get to the Confederates, and a jumpy Galveston Artillery Company gun crew at the San Luis Pass battery put two shots through the mainsail of the USS *Sam Houston*, a pilot boat that had been captured by the Union blockade.

Union forces didn't let this aggression go unchecked. The next day Captain James Alden steamed the *South Carolina* to the gun emplacement and exchanged fire with it for 30 minutes. Hundreds of spectators flocked to the beach to watch the fighting, and one of them was killed by an errant shell. The Confederates hit the *Carolina*'s hull three times and did

The old entry to the Episcopal Church.

minimal damage. The fighting ended when Alden ordered his men to steam back out into the Gulf. The skirmish helped the realists to convince the rest of the Confederate command that rather than commit any more of their already over-stretched troops to Galveston's defense, it was better to simply declare the city indefensible.

This led Confederate general Paul O. Hebert to withdraw all artillery and order an evacuation. It was rumored that interim Texas governor Edward Clark said he would burn the city to the ground rather than let the Union take it intact. Subsequent Texas wartime governors were equally zealous; Francis Lubbock, who replaced the defeated Edward Clark as governor in November 1861, interpreted Confederate conscription laws so that every able-bodied male between ages 16 and 60 was eligible for service. Soon, up to a quarter of Galveston's foreign-born male population was claiming citizenship in their native countries to avoid service. The fear of an attack drove many Galvestonians toward Houston and other inland cities; some of them did not return until the war was over.

The hostilities, combined with the exodus of residents, slowed Galveston's economy to a virtual standstill. Conditions between the soldiers and what remained of the civilian population rapidly declined. Workers refused to help the army with the evacuation, residents ambushed and killed soldiers, and soldiers lynched civilians. The commander of the military district of Galveston placed four guards at the door to every bar in the city, and when that didn't work he declared martial law.

Eventually, in October 1862, Federal forces did attack and occupy Galveston Island; however, the "second battle of Galveston," as it was called, was a nearly bloodless transfer. Prior to the actual landing of Union troops, Confederate forces evacuated the city and retreated to fortified positions on the mainland. Which meant that when Jonathan Wainwright, the commanding officer of the gunboat USS *Harriet Lane*, raised the American flag over the old U.S. Customs House, he was almost unopposed. Almost, because the Confederate battery at Fort Point, on Bolivar Peninsula, placed a shot across the *Harriet Lane*'s bow—which led Captain Wainwright to shell the battery into oblivion.

After taking the city, Union forces had to cope with an outbreak of yellow fever. Galveston remained in Union hands until New Year's Day 1863, when the Confederates mounted a late-night assault on the island. In a classic two-pronged attack that took advantage of the Union troops' low numbers—a fact that forced the occupiers to barricade themselves on the wharves and leave the remainder of the city undefended—Confederate infantry under the command of John Bankhead Magruder was brought by train across the trestle that connected Galveston to the mainland. The second prong involved cannon-carrying riverboats, piled high with protective cotton bales, to attack the Union naval vessels in the harbor.

The attack was a quick, clean Confederate victory. The *Harriet Lane* and three Union troop transports were captured; the USS *Westfield*, another gunboat, was run aground and exploded by her crew to prevent capture. Captain Wainwright and the senior Union officer, Commander William B. Renshaw, were both killed.

PRIVATIONS OF WAR

Union forces never tried to retake Galveston and instead focused on tightening the blockade. Blockade running continued, on a small scale, but there was no chance for trade to approach anything near its prewar volume. Galveston was too removed from the center of the conflict for it to be a Confederate priority, and as the war continued and the blockade's effectiveness increased, life in Galveston became more and more difficult.

Massive shortages of even the most basic necessities—food, fuel, medicine—coupled with currency devaluation, led to hyperinflation, with items like flour selling for $2 a pound and eggs at $4 a dozen. Coffee could fetch up to $20 a pound. This led most of the citizens and many of the troops to revert to a barter-based economy. As winter turned to spring and 1863 turned to 1864, conditions on the island worsened. In efforts to stave off hunger and cold, both the citizens and the soldiers resorted to tearing down fences, sheds, and abandoned buildings for use as firewood. Crime reached epidemic proportions, with theft, assault, and rape becoming routine. But the most pressing problem of the Confederate commander at Galveston, General James M. Hawes, wasn't the daily decline of the

city into anarchy; it was the high desertion rate among his troops. He tried to stem deser-
tions by ordering the military commissary to stop selling flour to the families of soldiers.
This myopic step led to a bread riot, in response to which Hawes issued an order declaring
Galveston "an entrenched camp."

This effectively placed the city under martial law, a decision that was made in haste but
one that proved to be correct. For that fall another epidemic of yellow fever swept through
the city, killing over 100 soldiers of the already-depleted garrison and an unknown number of civilians. It is possible that yellow fever came back to Galveston because ships
started to. In August, a few months before the yellow fever outbreak, Federal forces effectively closed one of the last commercially viable ports in the South—Mobile, Alabama. As
one of the few remaining deepwater ports in Confederate hands, Galveston took on a new
significance. In the preceding three years only 12 steam-powered blockade-runners had
entered the port; after the closing of Mobile, one entered every week, on average. Nevertheless, conditions in Galveston continued to deteriorate and didn't improve even when
Lee surrendered on April 9, 1865. The civilian population was so desperate that on May
24—the same day Federal forces boarded and burned the blockade runner *Denbigh*—a mob
of starving, poverty-stricken people boarded the stern-wheel paddle-steamer *Lark* and
stripped it of everything of any value. Eyewitnesses later recalled seeing "old women stag-
gering through the streets with sets of artillery harness and other plunder taken from the
vessel." When the crowd was through, the *Lark*'s captain took on the *Denbigh*'s crew and put
out to sea again, making it the last blockade-runner to clear a Confederate port.

POSTWAR CHAOS AND YANKEE RULE

Six days later the trans-Mississippi department of the Confederacy was surrendered. With
the removal of the last vestiges of Confederate authority, the entire state of Texas plunged
into chaos. Confederate soldiers disbanded without orders. Since many of them had not
been paid for months, and the ones who had been fortunate enough to get paid now found
Confederate money worthless, they began to engage in mass looting of public and private
property. The appeals of civilian and military leaders for loyalty and patriotism fell on deaf
ears, as most of the now-ex-soldiers adopted an every-man-for-himself attitude. More
than a few of them joined bands of armed highwaymen roaming throughout the state. In
addition to former Confederate soldiers, these bands were made up of some of the 6,000-
plus Union prisoners of war who had been held at the Ford and Groce prison camps in
northeast Texas. As the chaos spread so too did rumors that anyone who had played a sub-
stantial part in the affairs of Texas or the Confederacy would face harsh reprisal.

Fear of what a vengeful United States government would do and the refusal to live under
"Yankee rule" sent many fleeing across the
Mexican border. Among those who fled
were the majority of the civilian and military officials from the former government.
By the time provisional governor Andrew
Hamilton and General Granger, the newly
appointed commander of the department
of Texas, landed at Galveston with troops
on June 19, anarchy was near total.

The reading of the Emancipation Proclama-
tion on June 19 is commemorated each year
by Texas's black community with Juneteenth
celebrations. This annual tradition began
in Galveston in 1866 and quickly spread
throughout the state.

When Granger and Hamilton stepped onto the wharf at Galveston harbor, they were followed by five infantry companies, four of them white and one black. These "buffalo soldiers" were the first black troops seen in Texas, and their arrival didn't sit well with the residents. However, this was the least of Hamilton and Granger's problems, which included Indian raids on the western frontier, Mexican bandits attacking across the Rio Grande, and the lawlessness and chaotic financial situation virtually everywhere.

The first order of business for General Granger was raising the U.S. flag over Galveston Island to let what few residents remained know that Texas had been readmitted to the union, even if only provisionally. The second was freeing the slaves and finding some way to transition them into U.S. society at large. Overnight the black population of Galveston, and the rest of Texas, had gone from virtual serfdom to citizenship in an industrialized nation. This created problems that few could have predicted and even fewer could understand. Governor Hamilton's advice for the thousands of newly freed blacks was "Work hard and acquire property."

By the fall of 1865 some progress had been made—most notably the establishment of the Freedmen's Bureau, a government organization dedicated to educating and reintroducing former slaves into civil society. But the Freedmen's Bureau sparked an endless amount of contention and public animosity that made the education plan almost impossible to carry out. People were afraid to rent space for the schools; and if space could be found, people willing to take the position of teacher were just as rare. Even if teachers and space for the school could be found, money for textbooks and salaries was not available. Then there was the violence.

More than once the Freedmen's Bureau was unable to set up a school because of arson or threats of lynching. The amount of adversity faced by these schools required that they be set up in towns with a Federal garrison. This meant that Galveston had one of the first black schools in Texas.

Unfortunately, any accomplishments made by the new military government were quickly overshadowed by racial tension and problems between the civilian population, the provisional military government, and the civilian government.

The year 1867 also marked a return of yellow fever to the Galveston area. Still, this epidemic was nowhere near as bad as previous ones, due to the newly established Galveston Medical College.

RECOVERY AND NEW DISASTER

As reconstruction efforts faded with time, things gradually began returning to normal, so that by 1880 the economy had rebounded, and all seemed relatively stable as Galveston steamed into the 20th century. In 1897 the U.S. Army purchased 125 acres between 45th and 49th Streets to construct what was called a military reservation. Then 1900 came and brought with it a devastating hurricane, the likes of which have rarely been witnessed. The winds exceeded 120 miles per hour, and a storm surge of nearly 16 feet swept across the island, pushing a wall of debris at least two stories tall. An estimated six thousand people died, and perhaps thousands more, while a full quarter of the island was destroyed, including the still incomplete fort. The devastation of the island was legendary; the extreme eastern and western ends of the city were wiped clean. The middle of the city, from 9th to

A memorial to the 1900 hurricane.

45th Streets, suffered damage in a peculiarly angled pattern, and every structure within 15 blocks of the beach was flattened.

After officials were done calculating the losses, the members of the city government came to an ambitious conclusion: If the rebuilt city was going to survive, the island needed to be protected from future hurricanes. So the city began construction on a 15 1/2-foot-high, 10-mile-long seawall and the raising in elevation of 500 city blocks. While the construction of the seawall was carried out over a period of 60 years and at a cost of $16 million, the grade raising was completed in eight years. This monumental engineering feat required the raising of over 2,000 buildings on jacks and the construction of elevated wooden walkways between them. Beneath the now-elevated city a series of canals was constructed so that dredge barges could bring in 16 million cubic yards of sand from the bottom of Galveston Bay.

While the city of Galveston was being raised and the seawall constructed, the unfinished, unnamed military reservation between 45th and 49th Streets was turned over to the Army Corps of Engineers. Repairs and construction were finished relatively quickly, within 10 years, and the facility was christened Fort Crockett. Within a year of the last nail being driven, the U.S. Army's Coastal Artillery Corps had moved in. And none to soon, either, for those stationed at the fledgling fort soon found themselves thrust into preparations for "the Great War."

When the U.S. entered the First World War, Fort Crockett entered its heyday. Three thousand troops were stationed at Crockett, almost double the population of Galveston. They were there because of the large presence of Kaiser Wilhelm's submarines on the eastern seaboard. During the short amount of time the U.S. was involved in World War I, Fort Crockett was shipping out 100 to 200 artillery corps replacements a month. Mortar teams, railroad artillery companies, howitzer crews, fixed or field artillery batteries—all of them left from Galveston.

As thousands celebrated Armistice Day, it seemed like Galveston might be on its last legs. In 1914 the Houston Ship Channel had opened, sending the heavy tonnage and jobs inland, and now the end of the war meant the mothballing of Fort Crockett. As the Jazz Age dawned, the city was left struggling to find a way to survive. It turned to tourism and became one of the classiest resort destinations on the Gulf Coast. The shoreline was dominated by bathhouses, hotels, and nightclubs. Many compared it to Coney Island.

A battery at Fort Crockett.

Unfortunately, the good times wouldn't last. When World War II broke out, Galveston once again became an entrenched town.

U-BOATS AND POWs

As hard as it is now to imagine, from 1942 to 1943 German U-boats prowled the warm waters of the Gulf of Mexico. They sank 56 merchant ships and crippled 14 more. One boat, U-171, was even sighted in Galveston harbor on July 23, 1942. Fortunately for the city, the harbor was too shallow for any successful attacks in the area, which forced the German commander to move operations toward New Orleans. The sighting of U-171 and the unprecedented loss of shipping in the Gulf prompted the U.S. Army to finish the construction of the coastal artillery batteries on Galveston Island.

In addition to adding guns to the batteries, the army "casemated" one battery, adding a protective concrete and steel covering. The casemating was designed to withstand hits by 5,000-pound naval shells. It still stands to this day and now serves as the foundation for the San Luis Hotel.

Even though the guns at Fort Crockett were never used to destroy enemy ships, Galveston wasn't idle during the war. It was home to 650 German POWs up until 1946.

After the war, Galveston once more began to return to normal. The city reestablished

itself as one of the premiere resort destinations on the Gulf Coast, hosting such
legendary names as Frank Sinatra, Bob
Hope, Duke Ellington, and Jayne Mansfield. Fort Crockett even became a recreation center for army personnel. Sadly, the
era of Vegas-style glitz ended, and Galveston moved into a depression that lasted
decades. But some brilliant civic and commercial development helped pull the city
out of its doldrums.

Today's Galveston is a far cry from the
sandy wilderness of Cabeza de Vaca's time,
or even the young port city that Confederate and Union soldiers fought over; but

Lone Star Stalag
Between 1943 and 1945 more than 400,000
prisoners of war, most of them German,
were taken by Allied forces and sent to some
511 POW camps in the U.S. Historians are
unclear as to the number of prisoners that
wound up in the 70 POW camps throughout
Texas, but estimates range from 50,000 to
79,000. For further information regarding
German POWs in Texas, see Michael R.
Waters's fascinating book *Lone Star Stalag*,
published by Texas A&M University Press.

because of the strife and struggle of those who came before, each and every corner of
Galveston is haunted by the ghosts of human history. And Galvestonians are more than
happy to share that history with visitors. Just ask anyone you come across about the Great
Storm or Jean Laffite, and they'll give you an earful.

GETTING TO GALVESTON

Getting to Galveston is fairly simple; the city is an easy day trip from Houston.

By Car

Probably 99.9 percent of all visitors arrive in Galveston via automobile, and the drive is
fairly straightforward. There are three ways onto the island by car. The first is via
Interstate 45 and the Galveston Causeway, which becomes Broadway Street once it reaches
the city. The second is from the southwest via the San Luis Pass Bridge and FM 3005,
which eventually becomes Seawall Boulevard. The third is from the northeast via the
Bolivar Ferry—one of the two ferries in Texas. The Bolivar Ferry runs from the Bolivar
Peninsula to Galveston Island and deposits passengers on the east end of the island. It also
is worth mentioning that Galveston is one of the few cities in Texas that adheres strictly to
a grid-style layout. This means that the named/lettered streets run east to west and the
numbered streets run north to south.

By Bus or Train

Although there once was rail passenger service between Houston and Galveston, the last
train thundered down the tracks over 50 years ago. Recently there has been some discussion about reviving service, though it likely won't be happening anytime in the near future.
As for taking the bus to Galveston, the only line that runs to the city is Greyhound, and
service is not frequent. If you are going to take the bus to Galveston, call for availability and
schedule, and be forewarned that there is one Greyhound stop on the island with a ticket
window, and that is

Galveston Bus Station: 3825 Broadway, Suite B, Galveston, TX 77550; 409-765-7731 or
1-800-231-2222

By Air

While Galveston does have an airport, it is used primarily for charter and private flights, which means that for most visitors it is fairly unrealistic to try to fly into Galveston. The nearest major airports are Hobby and Bush in Houston, and flying into either of them will require a drive to Galveston. However, if you are flying a private plane, then the Galveston City Airport might be just what you are looking for.

There is a third possibility for flying into Galveston—Ellington Field—but it probably should be used as a last resort. Ellington is primarily a government facility; in fact it is where NASA houses the majority of its training aircraft, so getting clearance to land could prove tricky. However, it is home to the largest flying club in Texas and is used for the annual Wings Over Houston airshow, so it shouldn't be impossible.

Scholes International Airport at Galveston: 409-741-4609; www.galvestonairport.com; 2115 Terminal Dr., Galveston, TX

Ellington Field: 713-847-4200; 510 Ellington Field, Houston, TX 77034

By Boat

In the fall of 2000, Carnival Cruise Lines began operating out of a terminal on Galveston Island. This has made Galveston a very popular one-night stay for a lot of travelers and has led many hotels to offer cruise-ship specials. As other major cruise liners saw how profitable operating out of Galveston could be, they quickly climbed on board. Now four differ-

Cruise ships pull out of Galveston Harbor.

ent cruise lines (Carnival, Royal Caribbean, Princess, and Celebrity) all operate out of Galveston. If you are thinking of taking a cruise, check with the appropriate line to determine cost, departure date and time, and the requirements for boarding.

If you are planning on using your own boat to get to Galveston, you should know that it is entirely possible to sail into Galveston, which has many marinas and berths for pleasure boats. In fact, Galveston Bay is home to the third-largest concentration of pleasure boats in the United States, with many bars and restaurants maintaining their own private dock facilities. It should be noted that, except for the Houston Ship Channel, Galveston Bay is very shallow, with depths averaging 2–9 feet, and is filled with shell reefs along with oil and gas wells. This means that it is very necessary to purchase depth charts before attempting to sail in Galveston Bay.

GETTING AROUND GALVESTON

At a little over 3 miles wide and just under 30 miles long, Galveston isn't too terribly difficult to navigate. Interstate 45 and Galveston Bay are at the western end of the city (although the island itself stretches considerably farther west); Stewart Beach, Appfel Park and the Bolivar Ferry are at the eastern end. At the northern side is the harbor; at the southern is the seawall. The interior is a combination of shops and homes. The most famous area that combines both of these is the 30 blocks known as the Strand. This part of Galveston is bordered by Harborside on the north, Church Street on the south, 25th Street on the west, and 19th Street on the east. As you can see, getting around Galveston isn't all that difficult, for if you go in one direction long enough you'll inevitably hit water. However, walking can get rather old. Fortunately there are options.

Bicycle and Surrey Rentals

One of the most popular ways to get around on Galveston Island is renting a bicycle or a surrey—a four-seat pedal cab. This is perhaps one of the best ways to see the island. There are approximately half a dozen different companies that handle bike rentals in Galveston, almost all of them located on or near the seawall. Most of the companies rent bikes and surreys for the hour and the day. By far the largest bike rental company on the island is E-Z Rentals; they have three different locations, all of them along the seawall.

E-Z Rentals: 1020 Seawall Blvd., 409-766-7000; 1728 Seawall Blvd., 409-763-0705; 4712 Seawall Blvd., 409-765-7574

One of the most reputable bike rental companies in Galveston is Goody Rental. They have a reputation of treating the customer right.

Goody Rental: 2402 Seawall Blvd., 409-621-1062

Trolley Rides

Galveston is one of a handful of cities in the nation, and the only city in Texas, that still has streetcars. While the amount of ground covered by them is not as large as in San Francisco, they do provide a nice way to see the island. There are two trolley loops: the Downtown Loop and the Beach Loop. The Downtown Loop takes approximately 20 minutes to ride, and the Beach Loop takes 45. By transferring it is possible to ride the trolley from one end of the island to the other.

LODGING

Hotels

Galveston has many hotels in many different price ranges. Rather than fill up a guidebook with reviews of uninspiring accommodations, I thought it better to limit the listings to the best hotels I visited, which are these six.

GALVESTON ISLAND HILTON RESORT

409-744-5000 or 1-800-445-8667
www.galvestonhilton.com
5400 Seawall Blvd., Galveston, TX 77551
Price: Moderate
Credit Cards: AE, D, MC, V

The favorite hotel for those about to take one of the many cruises from Galveston, this particular Hilton brand hotel has more to offer than most of the chain, including a swim-up bar in the pool and great views of the beach.

HOLIDAY INN ON THE BEACH

409-740-3581
www.ichotelsgroup.com
5002 Seawall Blvd., Galveston, TX 77551
Price: Moderate
Credit Cards: AE, D, MC, V

Being a member of one of the largest and most recognizable hotel chains in the world should mean something. To some proprietors it doesn't, but to this hotel it does. The management really tries to live up to the slogan "Relax, it's Holiday Inn."

HOTEL GALVEZ

409-765-7721
www.wyndham.com
2024 Seawall Blvd., Galveston, TX 77550
Price: Expensive
Credit Cards: AE, DC, D, MC, and V

Opened in 1911, this palatial Victorian resort has for generations been called the Queen of the Gulf. Its marble bathrooms and rooms with hand-decorated walls have hosted such luminaries as Teddy Roosevelt, Howard Hughes, and Frank Sinatra. In the late 1980s the Galvez, along with most of the Texas coast, fell on hard times, and her beauty started to fade. However, Wyndham Hotels has just completed a $9 million restoration, which brought back the glitz and glamour—the columned and coffered Terrace Ballroom is outdone only by the 4,550-square-foot music hall. To keep pace with changing demands, there have also been some tasteful additions to the Galvez—it now offers a swim-up bar, Internet access, and cable TV.

MOODY GARDENS HOTEL

409-741-8484 or 1-888-388-8484
www.moodygardenshotel.com
7 Hope Blvd., Galveston, TX 77554
Price: Moderate to Expensive
Credit Cards: AE, D, MC, V

This multimillion-dollar hotel is the focal point of the 242-acre tourist mecca that is Moody Gardens. Everything about it, from the two-story lobby with a wall made entirely of glass, to the 500-square-foot guest rooms with three telephones and panoramic views (some complete with minibar and four-person Jacuzzi) sets this hotel apart from the pack. It offers fairly standard high-end amenities—gym, jogging track, pool, swim-up bar, business center, etc.—as well as some things fairly unusual for the pricey Galveston hotels, such as an interactive TV with video games, a private marina for the yacht and boat set, and self-parking—all presented in a family-friendly atmosphere that eschews Disneyland cartoon characters for a science-based experience.

The Shearn Moody Plaza is the last stop on many of Galveston's ghost tours.

SAN LUIS HOTEL

409-744-1500 or 1-800-445-0090
www.sanluisresort.com
5222 Seawall Blvd., Galveston, TX 77551
Price: Expensive
Credit Cards: AE, V, D, MC

One of Galveston's newer icons, the San Luis was built in 1984 on a World War II coastal artillery battery. It is considered by many to be one of the best resort destinations in Texas. It is 15 stories tall and has 244 rooms, each of which has its own private balcony that offers an unobstructed view of the Gulf. The San Luis also offers many amenities, such as his-and-her bathrobes, swim-up bar, turn-down service, private poolside cabanas, tennis courts, and just about everything you would expect from a top-of-the-line hotel.

TREMONT HOUSE

409-763-0300
www.wyndham.com
2300 Ship's Mechanic Row, Galveston, TX 77550
Price: Moderate to Expensive
Credit Cards: AE, V, MC, D

A three-star hotel with 102 Victorian-inspired rooms and 15 suites, the Tremont House was built in 1879 and completely refurbished in the late 1980s. It now includes almost all the usual amenities, including gym, bar/lounge, ballroom (across the street), 24-hour front desk, business center—plus a rooftop garden. This is one of the only hotels not right on the seawall, which can be good and bad, depending on what you are looking to do. Since it is located closer to the strand, it is next to the theatres and nightclubs, which can change the experience of the island. But then again it's not as though you would be far from the seawall and beach. It just won't be right across the street from you.

Bed & Breakfasts

At this writing Galveston Island has approximately 62 bed & breakfasts, which is quite a bit for a piece of land that is only 3 miles wide. Almost all these establishments offer the same amenities—thematically designed rooms, a large breakfast, and a personable owner who lives on site. These little touches make them among the best places to stay, primarily because the quality of your stay will always be high. Most of them come in around the $100-a-night range, with some getting into the $220-a-night range. However, you do get first-class service for that price.

AVENUE O BED AND BREAKFAST

409-762-2828 or 1-866-762-2868
www.avenueo.com
2323 Avenue O, Galveston, TX 77550
Price: Moderate to Expensive
Credit Cards: A, D, MC, V

A historic home on Galveston Island.

Built in 1923, this B&B is situated on one of the larger plots of land in Galveston, at a third of an acre. The fact that the house doesn't date to the Victorian era has allowed the owners to be a little more adventurous in their decor—they've added Polynesian elements to the antique/contemporary mix that dominates Galveston B&Bs. This is because the owners were bush pilots in America Samoa before coming to Galveston. Each room is a theme room, and the owners offer a good vegetarian breakfast and a lunch menu.

COASTAL DREAMS BED & BREAKFAST
409-770-0270 or 1-866-770-0270
www.coastaldreamsbnb.com
3602 Avenue P, Galveston, TX 77550
Price: Expensive to Very Expensive

This is possibly the most tricked-out B&B on Galveston Island, which means that it has almost all the basic amenities of a two-to two-and-a-half-star hotel. Things like wireless Internet, central air/heat, a pool and hot tub, cable TV in every room, DVD/VCR in every room, ultrasoft Egyptian cotton towels, and a BBQ pit definitely help to round out the experience. The food is also good.

COPPERSMITH INN BED & BREAKFAST
409-763-7004 or 1-800-515-7444
www.coppersmithinn.com
1914 Avenue M, Galveston, TX 77550
Price: Expensive to Very Expensive
Credit Cards: A, D, MC, V

Built in 1887 from renowned German architect Alfred Muller's designs, the Coppersmith is fairly unusual among Galveston B&Bs in that all the guest rooms are not in one building. Behind the main house are two cottages, which are the true gems of the place, especially Clara's Country Cottage. This outbuilding has a double-bed loft and antique tin bathtub. Another nice feature is that the Coppersmith loans bicycles to its guests. And the seawall is only six blocks away. A traditional country breakfast is offered.

GARDEN INN
409-770-0592 or 1-888-720-7298
1601 Ball St., Galveston, TX 77550
www.galveston.com/gardeninn
Price: Moderate to Expensive
Credit Cards: MC, V

One of the things that distinguish B&Bs from regular hotels is how much they reflect the personality of the owner. Owners Pam and Mike Gilbert purchased the Garden Inn in 2000 and have made it a family-friendly establishment, with a focus on local history and plants. They also offer loaner bikes for their guests.

GRACE MANOR BED AND BREAKFAST
409-621-1662 or 1-800-810-8590
1702 Postoffice St., Galveston, TX 77550
www.gracemanor-galveston.com
Price: Expensive to Very Expensive
Credit Cards: A, DC, D, MC, V

One of the more picturesque buildings on the island, stately Grace Manor was built in 1905 and is run by one very nice lady. She will even serve you homemade cookies before bed and has a sweet dog named Gracie. She has no problems adjusting your checkout time if you have a dinner engagement planned. The four rooms all are tastefully decorated with antiques and king-size beds, and one has its own patio. Grace Manor is within walking distance of the Strand and a two-minute car ride to the seawall.

INN AT 1816 POSTOFFICE
409-765-9444 or 1-888-558-9444
1816 Postoffice St., Galveston, TX 77550
www.inn1816postoffice.com
Price: Moderate to Expensive
Credit Cards: A, D, MC, V

This quaint little four-room inn was a private house until 1995, when it was acquired by a group of four friends. They've spent the last decade restoring the building and adding antique furniture. The thing that really separates this B&B from the others on the island is its terrace-style porches. A staple in southern antebellum architecture, they were the place to sit and watch the sunset. They still are. Fortunately these have been painstakingly restored to their former glory.

ISLAND JEWEL BED & BREAKFAST
409-763-5395 or 1-866-428-5395
www.islandjewelbnb.com
1725 Avenue M, Galveston, TX 77550
Price: Expensive
Credit Cards: MC, V

Billed as the perfect destination for the gay and gay-friendly traveler, the Island Jewel was listed by *OutSmart Magazine* Houston as the best B&B in 2006. Admittedly it is a little small, at only three rooms, each of which is themed around a specific precious stone. The diamond room is gorgeous in a country-manner style.

LONE PALM BED AND BREAKFAST
409-762-4867
2214 Avenue M, Galveston, TX 77550
Price: Expensive to Very Expensive
Credit Cards: MC, V

This out-of-the-way B&B tends to get overlooked by most people looking to spend the night on the island. Which is a shame, because they have a helpful and knowledgeable staff that will treat you like family and answer any and all questions you have. The owner takes pride in making sure your experience is the best. The location makes for a bit of a hike to the Strand or the seawall, although for cyclists it should pose no problem.

QUEEN ANNE BED AND BREAKFAST
409-497-4936 or 1-866-435-1905
www.galvestonqueenanne.com
1915 Sealy St., Galveston, TX 77550
Price: Moderate to Expensive
Credit Cards: A, D, MC, V

One of the most recognized B&Bs in the state of Texas, the Queen Anne is a favorite for travelers, so much so that it has been rated as one of the 10 best in the country. With six guest rooms, the Queen Anne features a seamless blend of the past and the present; the antique furnishings and Jacuzzi bathtubs don't seem to clash at all. It must be the exposed brickwork that ties it all together, or maybe it's the chamois curtains.

A VICTORIAN BED & BREAKFAST INN
409-762-3235
www.vicbb.com
511 17th St., Galveston, TX 77550

Price: Expensive to Very Expensive
Credit Cards: AE, MC, V

The Victorian claims to be the island's first B&B, and its impressive structure, with stately porches, indeed dates back to the beginning of the 20th century. It offers three suites: Zacary's, Mauney's, and the Garden Apartment. The last is perfect for romantic interludes. Each suite comes with its own private bath. There are also three king-size bedrooms, which share a centrally located bath.

VILLA BED & BREAKFAST
409-766-1722 or 866-618-1723
www.thevillabedandbreakfast.com
1723 25th St., Galveston, TX 77550
Price: Moderate to Expensive
Credit Cards: MC, V

The decor and intimacy of this charming converted home make it seem like it should be in the south of Europe, not South Texas. In the city's Silk Stocking District, the house was built in 1914. The three bedrooms—the Bordeaux Room, Cote d'Azur Room, and the Provence Room—all come with their own bath and antique furnishings. There's also an enclosed patio, a trolley stop on the corner, and a fantastic view of the Mardi Gras parade. The prices of the rooms vary along with the decor.

Vacation Rentals
Galveston vacation properties vary widely and can be rented for anywhere from one night to six months. Many are handled by brand-name real estate agencies, others by individual owners. Many properties are available each year throughout the island, and as with any rentals, problems can come up—difficult landlords, tacky decor, lack of a central location, maintenance responsibilities, and price are only some of the factors you should weigh before

Snowbirds

Winter Texans, or snowbirds as they are sometimes called, are a particular subset of people who have moved to Texas. They are generally retired northerners who find that as they have grown older they can't take the cold as well as they used to. Often times they rent property or live in RVs on the Texas coast from late fall to late spring. Strange as it may seem, this group of people is almost universally revered by coastal residents—not just because of the money they bring to the local economy in the traditionally slow winter months, but because they are almost always some of the nicest people on the coast.

going down this route. If you are considering renting a beach house for a weekend or a week, do your homework. Prices of properties on the same block can differ by thousands of dollars; the cost of renting the same property can change from month to month or in some cases day to day. The uncertainty involved in vacation rentals is something that can send many people scurrying back to hotels. However, if you do wish to continue on this path, the companies listed below are a good place to start. They are all very reputable, and most of them are open to negotiation.

CASTAWAYS RESORT PROPERTIES
409-737-5300 or 1-800-380-5100
www.castawaysgroup.com
11132 FM 3005, Galveston, TX 77550

COBB REAL ESTATE
409-684-3790 or 1-800-880-2622
www.cobbrealestate.com
Hwy. 87 and Sand Piper, Crystal Beach, TX 77550

THE GALVESTONIAN
409-765-6161 or 1-888-526-6161
1401 E. Beach Dr., Galveston, TX 77550

SAND 'N SEA PIRATES BEACH
409-737-2556 or 1-800-880-2554
www.sandnsea.com
4127 Pirate's Beach / 13706 FM 3005, Galveston, TX 77550

WOLVERTON & ASSOCIATES REALTY
409-737-1430 or 1-800-445-1396
www.wolvertonrealty.com
17614 San Luis Pass Rd., Galveston, TX 77550

Camping and RV Parks
Camping in Galveston? Most people who vacation in Galveston wouldn't dream of camping. But then again there are those who like to rough it. While Galveston may not be the ideal place to camp, and there are very few facilities for it, what the island lacks in open spaces it makes up for in accessibility.

BAYOU SHORES RV RESORT
409-744-2837 or 1-888-744-2837
www.bayoushoresrvresort.com
E-mail: bonthb@sbcglobal.net
6310 Heards Lane, Galveston, TX 77551
Price: Moderate
Credit Cards: D, MC, V

This is one of the larger RV parks in Galveston. It has 84 full-hookup lots, a restaurant and bar on site, laundry room, copy service, fishing pier, boat ramp, and all sorts of other things to make you feel welcome. It should be noted that unlike some RV parks, this one is for RVs only; there is no place to pitch a tent. They also aren't on the beach; they are on the bay. They do, however, offer daily, weekly, and monthly rates, honor all major discounts, and are a member of the Galveston Winter Texan Association.

DELLANERA RV PARK
409-797-5102 or 1-888-425-4753 x102
www.galveston.com/dellanera/reserve.html
E-mail: dellanera@galvestonparkboard.org
10901 San Luis Pass Rd., Galveston, TX 77554
Price: Moderate
Credit Cards: AE, D, MC, V

This park is run by the Galveston Park Board of Trustees, and it shows. It has almost all the amenities anyone could want from an RV park: 1,000 feet of beach, paved parking spots, 63 full hook-ups (all of which are 50 amp) and 21 partials, picnic sites, and a pavilion with showers, laundry facilities, gift shop, and rec room. To make things even better, the Galveston Park Board of Trustees just completed the construction of 12 new spaces. These new spaces are all pull-throughs and were built for expandable trailers and motor homes. They also feature their own picnic tables and landscaping. Two more perks are that Dellanera accepts checks and provides free WiFi for guests.

GALVESTON ISLE RV RESORT
409-744-5464
2323 Skymaster Rd., Galveston, TX 77554

Located on the western end of the island, this simple and unassuming RV park is literally minutes from some of the bigger draws. Schlitterbahn, Moody Gardens, and the Lone Star Flight Museum are all within a mile of the campground. The staff and permanent guests are all very helpful and friendly. While this may lack some of the amenities of larger parks, like say a KOA, it does offer a nice quiet place to relax after a long day of driving.

RESTAURANTS

The name Galveston will always be synonymous with seafood. And rightly so, given the city's island location and its proximity to New Orleans, the fountainhead of Gulf Coast cooking. And while Galveston is justly recognized throughout the state as the place to get great seafood, it has much more to offer than just fish and shrimp. As the island's population has changed, so have the restaurants. Now it's possible to get food from five different continents with some of the freshest ingredients imaginable, and almost all of it is available every day.

APACHE MEXICAN CUISINE
409-765-5646
511 20th St., Galveston, TX 77550
Type of Food: Mexican
Price: Inexpensive to Moderate
Credit Cards: AE, D, MC, V

Apache is a fairly typical *taqueria*. While the menu includes the traditional Tex-Mex fare of burritos and enchiladas, it also has some more authentic dishes like *calabaza con pollo*, which is squash with chicken, and *fideo con carne*, aka vermicelli with beef, and chicken *mole*. This is a local favorite for happy-hour margaritas.

BENNO'S ON THE BEACH
409-762-4621
1200 Seawall Blvd., Galveston TX 77550
Credit Cards: AE, D, MC, V
Type of Food: Seafood
Price: Inexpensive to Moderate

A mid-scale family-oriented eatery, Benno's offers Gulf Coast seafood at low prices with no vegetarian alternatives. All meals come with a variation on the classic fries/hush puppies theme. The menu is classic Texas seafood—shrimp, oysters, and crab, all fried or stuffed. This is most

Fullen's Waterwall

definitely a lunch establishment that is also open for dinner.

BISTRO LECROY

409-762-4200
2021 Strand, Galveston,TX 77550
Type of Food: Louisiana/Creole
Price: Moderate to Expensive
Credit Cards: AE, D, MC, V

This phenomenal New Orleans–style restaurant serves some of the best crab cakes this side of the Sabine River. The decor is tastefully muted, the service excellent, and the location perfect. Ask the waiter about the history of the building; it makes for an interesting story to listen to while rehydrating from the stroll down the Strand. This is truly a superb restaurant.

CLARY'S SEAFOOD RESTAURANT

409-740-0771
8509 Teichman Rd., Galveston, TX 77550
Type of Food: Seafood
Price: Moderate to Expensive
Credit Cards: AE, D, MC, V

Clary's *is* Galveston seafood, the good and the bad. When Clary's is good it's great—the soft-shell crab that is worth calling ahead for, homemade salad dressing, and Creole seasoning make you wonder why you have never heard of the place before. Although Clary's also has its off days. Fortunately the hits outweigh the misses by a 5:1 ratio.

FULLEN'S WATERWALL

409-765-6787
2110 Strand, Galveston, TX 77550
Type of Food: Burgers
Price: Inexpensive
Credit Cards: AE, D, MC, V

The menu is quintessential Texan burgers—everything from a straight-up hamburger to a tuna burger. It deviates very little from the burger-joint formula by offering minimal vegetarian alternatives and a small selection of domestic beer. It is lovely to rest in the courtyard, watch the shade trees sway in the wind, and listen to the street musicians play.

GAIDO'S FAMOUS SEAFOOD RESTAURANT

409-762-9625 or 1-800-525-0064
3802 Seawall Blvd., Galveston, TX 77550
Type of Food: Seafood
Price: Expensive
Credit Cards: AE, D, MC, V

Gaido's is one of the most famous and notorious restaurants in Galveston. Founded as a sandwich shop in 1911 at Murdoch's Bath House by San Jacinto Gaido, it has been managed by four generations of the Gaido family. With hundreds

Cajun vs. Creole

Most people know that Louisiana has produced two schools of cooking: the Cajun style and the Creole style. But few people know that the two types of cooking reflect two radically different social classes, with radically different histories and experiences. To understand the extreme variations in the cuisine, you have to understand the history of the two groups. First, the Cajuns—or Acadians, as they prefer to be called—were French colonists who had settled in Acadia (now Nova Scotia) in the early 1600s. Throughout the 17th century Acadia was a political football kicked and passed back and forth between France and England through various wars and treaties. Finally in 1713, in the Treaty of Utrecht, most of what is now Nova Scotia was handed over to the British permanently. This left some six to ten thousand French-speaking Acadians up the proverbial creek. The British government didn't trust them and in fact saw them as a potential French fighting force. For the next 40 years the British would make the Acadians swear loyalty oaths on a semiregular basis, and neither side thought much of it, until the French and Indian War. When the British attacked Fort Beauséjour in 1755, they found 200 Acadians mixed in with the garrison. The British saw this as validation of their worst fears—however, the Acadians claimed they had been forced into fighting for the French. The British didn't care; they rounded up approximately three-quarters of the Acadian population, forced them onto ships, and dispersed them throughout the globe. In what has came to be called the Great Upheaval, some of the Acadians went to Georgia, where they were sold into slavery, others went back to France, where they were treated as pariahs, and many of them went to Louisiana, where they were sent to live in the humid marshlands of the bayous with the Indians. It was here that they found a new home and created a new cuisine. It is a cuisine of adaptation and survival forged in the backwoods. It was here that the Acadians befriended the Indians who introduced them to new plants and spices. It was here that they hunted rabbits and frogs and fished for crawdads and catfish and added these new meats to their traditional recipes. They took these disparate ingredients and with love, ingenuity, and resolve threw them all into the only cooking pot the family was able to save from the houses the English set fire to in the woods of Acadia.

If the experiences of the Cajuns—the flight from persecution and the struggle to survive—marks their cuisine, then the lives of luxury, longing for old Europe, and the melting pot of New Orleans are what are reflected in Creole cooking. The Louisiana Creoles were the second and third sons and daughters—the ones who didn't inherit the family estate and titles—of the European aristocracy. They came to the New World in the early 1700s to establish themselves, and they brought with them the desire for the lifestyle of the landed gentry they had known. The Creole culture reflects this, from the music to the art to the food. Creole cooking is founded on classic French recipes that were brought to the New World by wives and cooks. Early in the history of colonization these culinary pioneers grew frustrated by the fact that they simply couldn't get the ingredients they were used to, so they were forced to modify the recipes to include what was available. The modifications came to include borrowing ingredients from their Spanish hosts—Louisiana was a Spanish colony after the British defeated the French in the Seven Years War—as well as cooking techniques from the Haitian and west African slaves and spices from the Indians. To run the risk of gross oversimplification, Cajun food is the food of the 18th-century Louisianan proletariat, while Creole is the bourgeois counterpart.

of historic pictures and menus on display, the decor reflects this long history. The house specials are just as well-known, especially the whole stuffed flounder. This is a deboned flounder, stuffed with a seasonal seafood dressing, basted with lemon garlic butter, and broiled to perfection. Another favorite is Snapper Fritz, a fillet of fresh-off-the-boat Gulf red snapper that's charcoal grilled and then topped with jumbo lump crabmeat that has been sautéed in lemon butter.

JUJU'S HANGOUT & BAR
409-765-9300
2408 Strand at 24th St., Galveston, TX 77550
Type of Food: Pub grub
Price: Inexpensive to Moderate
Credit Cards: AE, D, MC, V

Juju's can best be described as Galveston's homegrown Hooters, with Playstations for kids. The "Juju girls" are always trying to keep the party going, the menu is typical Texas pub grub (burgers, nachos, and the like) and the clientele is the local frat-boy set. Don't be surprised if a limbo contest or conga line breaks out while you're here. They also have live music on Saturday nights and Sunday afternoons.

LA ESTACION
409-762-4262
2428 Ball St., Galveston, TX 77550
Type of Food: Mexican/breakfast
Price: Inexpensive
Credit Cards: AE, D, MC, V

This is one of the best breakfast locations on the island, and everybody knows it. They serve the biggest breakfast burritos in town; their tortillas have been described as hand-towel size. Their *migas* are also worth a try. It can also get fairly crowded, and the lunch menu doesn't stand up to the well-deserved praise of the breakfasts.

LUIGI'S RISTORANTE ITALIANO
409-763-6500
2328 Strand at Tremont (23rd), Galveston, TX 77550
Type of Food: Italian
Price: Moderate to Expensive
Credit Cards: AE, D, MC, V

Located in the historic Sealy-Hutchings Building, Luigi's marks the first solo effort of chef Luigi Ferre. The black trim gives a modern feel to the casual trattoria decor, and a menu heavy on Italian favorites, combined with a truly helpful staff, makes this charming bistro a local favorite. Dishes like *rotolo di mare*, which is a pasta roll stuffed with asparagus, shrimp, and crabmeat, make full use of the proximity to the Gulf. Reservations are suggested, if not required. For a truly memorable experience, make arrangements to sit at the chef's table in the kitchen. If you do, you'd better bring your appetite, since you'll be getting a specially prepared five-course meal.

MARIO'S SEAWALL ITALIAN RESTAURANT
409-763-1693
628 Seawall Blvd., Galveston, TX 77551
Type of Food: Italian
Price: Inexpensive
Credit Cards: AE, D, MC, V

When New Jersey transplants Antonio and Nilda Smecca acquired Mario's in 1973 it was already well-known for its "flying pizzas." The Smeccas immediately began to turn a moderately successful eatery into a statewide destination. One of the first things they did was to improve on the hand-tossed pizzas. While Antonio was mastering the art of pizza aerobics, Nilda was teaching the kitchen staff how to make American-style Italian food. The Smeccas' pizza had such a reputation on the island that the couple's two sons, Johnny and Joey, started their own pizza place and parlayed the success of that venture into the Galveston Restaurant Group, an acquisitions and development company that has allowed them to become some of the most powerful players in the Galveston restaurant industry.

MOSQUITO CAFÉ

409-763-1010
www.mosquitocafe.com
628 14th St., Galveston, TX 77550
Type of Food: Contemporary cuisine
Price: Inexpensive to Moderate
Credit Cards: AE, D, MC, V

This is one of Galveston's most recent additions, having opened in 1999, and one of its best. If you are tired of the hush puppy, fried shrimp, fish po-boy selections of other restaurants, the Mosquito is the place for you. With a menu that focuses on grilled, roasted, and sautéed fare, along with deep bowls of pasta, lots of vegetarian options, and a friendly and helpful staff that knows what focaccia bread is, this little bastion of urbanity is a welcome respite on the island. The Mosquito opted for clean, modern lines and an airy, sunlit dining room. One of the things that helps set the Mosquito apart from other international/eclectic bistros is its attention to detail, such as including a kid's menu. Instead of passively discouraging younger diners, the Mosquito welcomes them. It is this attitude that has gotten them 28 positive reviews, in everything from the *Galveston County Daily News* to the Zagat Survey.

OLYMPIA GRILL

409-766-1222
www.olympiagrill.net
4908 Seawall Blvd., Galveston, TX 77550
Type of Food: Greek
Price: Inexpensive to Moderate
Credit Cards: AE, D, MC, V

The only Greek restaurant on Galveston

One difference that the Greeks bring to wine-making is pine resin. One famous type of Greek wine, retsina, was originally aged in amphorae, or ceramic vases, sealed with pine resin. The functional aspect of the pine resin was to make the amphorae airtight, but it also imparted a distinctive piney taste that is associated to this day with Greek wine.

Isle that's actually owned by Greeks, the Olympia boasts a healthy wine list—and it's almost exclusively Greek wines. They also offer over a dozen seafood dishes, as well as a healthy amount of vegetarian plates.

PALMS M&M

409-766-7170
2401 Church St., Galveston, TX 77550
Type of Food: Gourmet
Price: Expensive
Credit Cards: AE, D, MC, V

This is a high-class, high-price steak and seafood restaurant with a menu that reads like a who's who of famous dishes. Covering everything from ceviche (raw fish marinated in lime juice and served with onion, tomatoes, olives, capers, and jalapeños) to Kobe steak (supposedly the most tender and succulent steak on the planet) M&M's menu is awe-inspiring. It is worth noting that M&M is the only place on Galveston Island, and one of the very few places in the Houston-Galveston area, that serves Kobe steak. The appearance of such an international delicacy is not as unusual as it may seem, considering that many of the dishes on the menu are Asian in inspiration, if not in origin. The marinated baby octopus, listed as Zuka Ika (served with a seaweed salad and *tobikko*, which is flying-fish roe) clearly wasn't created in Texas. The diversity of the menu actually makes the restaurant more interesting, even if the prices are daunting.

PAPA'S GOURMET PIZZA AND SUBS

409-766-7272
4400 Seawall Blvd., Galveston, TX 77550
Type of Food: American-Italian
Price: Inexpensive
Credit Cards: AE, D, MC, V

Started in 1997 by Johnny and Joey
Smecca, sons of Antonio and Nilda of
Mario's fame, Papa's is a pretty standard
pizza, sandwich, and Italian food eat
in/delivery service. The prices are more
than competitive with the big chains, and
the food is better.

PHO 20

409-750-9200
3728 Broadway, Galveston, TX
Type of Food: Vietnamese

Price: Inexpensive
Credit Cards: AE, D, MC, V

The food is phenomenal. The spring rolls,
pan-seared egg noodles, hard tofu dishes
(a thicker type of tofu than most places),
pho, and café sudat are all excellent and
extremely affordable.

PHOENIX BAKERY & COFFEE SHOP

409-763-4611
2228 Ships Mechanic Row at 23rd St.,
Galveston, TX 77550
Type of Food: Contemporary/breakfast
Price: Inexpensive
Credit Cards: AE, D, MC, V

The Phoenix is one of the best-kept breakfast and lunch secrets on the island and
has a thoroughly modern menu—no bacon,
eggs, and grits here. The fruit plate served
with fresh banana nut bread, homemade
breakfast burritos, and delicious beignets
all go well with their exceptional and always good coffee. Sadly, they only keep
breakfast and lunch hours and close at 5 PM
Monday through Saturday and 4 PM on
Sunday.

QUEEN'S BAR-B-QUE

409-762-3151
35th St. and Avenue S, Galveston, TX 77550
Type of Food: Barbecue
Price: Inexpensive
Credit Cards: AE, D, MC, V

Voted Best Bar-B-Que by the *Galveston
County Daily News* and by Galveston.com &
Company in 2003, Queen's serves traditional Texas barbecue in a very traditional
setting. The wood-paneled walls are lined
with photos of Little League teams that the
restaurant sponsored. The thing that sets
Queen's apart from the crowd is the inclu-
sion of two unexpected items: a superb
French dip and an even better "BQ Tejas
Chicken Cordon Bleu," which comes on a
toasted sourdough bun covered in "BQ
sauce." It should be mentioned that Texas

BBQ chefs tend to use a much sweeter sauce than chefs in many parts of the country and tend to use a lot more of it. This makes the act of eating Texas BBQ a rather messy affair.

RAINFOREST CAFÉ
409-744-6000
5310 Seawall Blvd., Galveston, TX 77550
Type of Food: American
Price: Moderate to Expensive
Credit Cards: AE, D, MC, V

This is one of the 875 restaurants owned by Tillman Fertitta, the man who happens to be Texas's biggest restaurateur. It includes animatronic animals, a river adventure ride, gift shop, jungle plants, and a "magic mushroom" bar that features carved animal stools. The dishes have colorful names like Leaping Lizard Lettucewraps, Rasta Pasta, and Congo Catfish. The Rainforest is the only restaurant concept at all U.S. and foreign Disney locations. Tillman Fertitta has also expanded this concept into Mexico, Canada, China, and Europe.

RUDY & PACO'S
409-762-3696
2020 Postoffice St. at 20th, Galveston, TX 77550
Type of Food: Central / South American
Price: Moderate to Expensive
Credit Cards: AE, D, MC, V

This Central / South American steak and seafood restaurant specializes in many things you won't find anywhere else on Galveston—like a dress code. Fried plantains with homemade salsa appetizer, tuna with jalapeño cream sauce, and plantain crusted chicken are just some of the dishes worth sampling. The margaritas are excellent, and the wait staff knows exactly which of the many wines in Rudy and Paco's ample cellar will perfectly complement your meal.

SALTWATER GRILL
409-762-3474
2017 Postoffice St. at 21st Galveston, TX 77550
Type of Food: Gourmet seafood
Price: Moderate
Credit Cards: AE, D, MC, V

Under the tenure of adventuresome executive chef Chris Lopez, who believes in capitalizing on the bounties of the Gulf, the Saltwater Grill has become one of the hottest restaurants in the most competitive seafood market in the state. The fact that the menu is printed up daily indicates the presence of some of the freshest seafood in the Houston-Galveston area. Take all that and add a location just minutes away from the Grand 1894 Opera House and blocks from the Strand, plus their hand-rolled-sushi Sundays, and you have an equation that results in the dining room being usually packed with repeat customers. Even the local hotel staffs recommend the place to guests. Reservations are often the best bet.

SHRIMP N' STUFF
409-763-2805
39th St. at Avenue O, Galveston, TX 77550
Type of Food: Seafood
Price: Inexpensive
Credit Cards: AE, D, MC, V

The name says it all: This is a Shrimp Restaurant. Like most places on the Texas Gulf Coast, they serve shrimp three ways—boiled, fried, and stuffed—and in three different sizes—5-, 8-, and 12- piece dinners. What the menu lacks in variety—when it says fish it means catfish and catfish only—it more than makes up for in value. The best deal is to get the po-boy combination, any two of their delicious seafood po-boys for a little more than the price of one. This allows two people to eat well for less than $6. Throw in fries and a couple of drinks and you might spend eight bucks. It'll make a nice lunch, especially if you're on a budget.

THE SPOT

409-621-5237
3204 Seawall Blvd., Galveston, TX 77550
Type of Food: American
Price: Inexpensive
Credit Cards: AE, D, MC, V

The Spot is known as one thing: a great place to take young children. With an on-site ice cream parlor and dessert bakery, no kid can resist, and a plus for the adults is the on-site bar.

SUNFLOWER BAKERY

409-763-5500
1527 Church St. at 15th, Galveston, TX 77550
Type of Food: Sandwiches
Price: Inexpensive
Credit Cards: AE, D, MC, V

This is a favorite local lunch spot. The sandwiches are great, the croissants are a winner, and the soup and desserts are also good. Be sure to try the tomato basil soup and chocolate pecan pie. As for drinks, definitely try the strawberry lemonade, although be forewarned, it is a bit sweet.

YAMATO JAPANESE SEAFOOD SUSHI & STEAKHOUSE

409-744-2742
2104 61st St., Galveston, TX 77550
Type of Food: Japanese
Price: Moderate to Expensive
Credit Cards: AE, D, MC, V

For almost 20 years the chefs at this Galveston legend have been wowing locals and tourists with their fantastic knife work and exquisitely prepared dishes. In addition to good sushi they offer exquisitely prepared filet mignon and lobster. And since all entrées come with miso soup and fried rice, this Japanese-American fusion restaurant allows for the best of the Orient and the West.

NIGHTLIFE

It should be noted that not all clubs are open every day of the week, and the best ones usually aren't easy to find.

BALINESE ROOM

409-762-9696
www.balineseroom.net
2107 Seawall Blvd., Galveston, TX 77550

The Balinese Room was named Texas's "Night Club of the Century" in the December 1999 issue of *Texas Monthly*, beating out Gilley's, the honky-tonk immortalized in *Urban Cowboy*, and for good reason. There are few venues in Texas as storied as the Balinese. Built by the Maceo brothers in the early forties, the Balinese hosted everyone—Frank Sinatra, Groucho Marx, Bob Hope, and Tony Bennett, just to name a few. It was one of the few desegregated clubs in the South, which meant that giants like Duke Ellington could play the same stage as his white counterparts; and since the club was some 600 feet out into the Gulf, the bar staff had ample warning of any police raids—something that was to prove very useful for the Maceo brothers' other source of income: illegal casino-style gambling. When the Texas Rangers would storm the Balinese, the bartenders would simply fold the gaming tables into the dance floor. Another claim to fame is that the Balinese Room is *the* birthplace of the margarita. In 1948 head bartender Santos Cruz invented the drink for singer Peggy (Margaret) Lee. After a thorough restoration, the Balinese reopened in 1997 with the addition of a café, photography studio, gift shop and museum, hair salon, and glass-bottomed massage therapy room so that clients can view the ocean as their tensions are rubbed away. This club also has an interesting footnote for Sinatra-philes: The main walkway contains an original oil painting Frank did in 1942.

CABANA CLUB
409-763-9574
817 21st St., Galveston, TX 77550

Despite its touristy name, this is most definitely not the type of bar you just walk into. It helps to know someone, especially during Kappa Beach Party. Since this bar caters exclusively to Galveston's small and insular hip-hop set, it can be fairly hard to get into when the big names come down and hang out each spring.

COCKTAILS
409-762-7900, reservations 409-599-4169
2411 Mechanic St., Galveston, TX 77550

Since it is the only place on Galveston Island with karaoke six nights a week and a live performance stage that features music and theater, Cocktails can be somewhat confusing. Which is why the demure patio bar is refreshing—with a gently babbling fountain, nice low lights, and proximity to the two biggest theaters on Galveston Island, it can function as the perfect place to wind down the evening or get it started. This is the type of place to go to if you don't mind doing your drinking from a Dixie cup.

JAVA'S 213
409-762-5282
213 Tremont (23rd St.), Galveston, TX 77550

Considered by many to be the oldest coffee shop on Galveston Island, Java's got its start in the early 1990s' Gen-X coffee craze and has kept going. In fact almost every-thing about it screams '90s alterna-cul-

The only skyscraper on Galveston is lit up on a foggy night.

ture, from the midweek poetry reading to the once-a-month jam session / drum circle. That plus the cheap drinks makes it one of the regular hangouts for Galveston's bohemian set—what few of them there are. One of the main problems with this place is that it closes early, midnight Monday through Saturday and 10 PM on Sundays.

THE LOUNGE
409-763-1000
2410 Strand, Galveston, TX 77550

The only dance club on Galveston Island, the Lounge bills itself as "Galveston's only Ultra-Lounge"—whatever that means. Since it is patterned after Miami clubs, the Lounge tends toward artifice and girls in skin-tight revealing clothes. Whether this one bar will radically alter the nightlife of this sleepy beachfront community, changing it into something that will rival South Beach or Manhattan, remains to be seen.

MARKET STREET TAVERN
409-762-8099
2310 Market St., Galveston, TX 77550

This is a slightly schizophrenic club. It can't decide whether it wants to be a dance club, an arcade, or a sports bar. On the plus side, it does have a halfway decent light show, a passable selection of standard import beers, and some classic video games.

MOLLY'S IRISH PUB
409-763-4466
2013 Postoffice St., Galveston, TX 77550

Ask anyone in Houston between the ages of 21 and 35 to name a Galveston bar, and chances are they'll say Molly's. This Irish-themed pub has cold beer, dark wood walls, and is known as the best bar in Galveston. It is small and, like all good bars, at times can feel like a clubhouse.

OLD CELLAR BAR
409-763-4477
2015 Postoffice St., Galveston, TX 77550

This is a very trendy after-work / happy-hour bar with a fine selection of scotch and wine, though the crowds can be a little thick at times and the drinks just a wee bit pricey. It also boasts one of the most artfully done interiors around.

OLD QUARTER ACOUSTIC CAFÉ
409-762-9199, 409-737-4915
413 20th St., Galveston, TX 77550

Possibly the most famous live music venue on Galveston Island, the Old Quarter and its owner Wrecks Bell are legends in the Texas music world. This is an anchor in the acoustic guitar singer-songwriter tour circuit, which means that almost all the music is very well played, very well sung, and very folky. Thursday is open-mike night, where you are likely to hear aspiring singer-songwriters working out new material. Sometimes it can be a challenging process to watch, but since the drinks are normally moderately priced and the crowd is also a little older, 35 and up, the musicians often find the groove pretty quickly and make some great music.

O'MALLEY'S STAGE DOOR PUB
409-763-1731
2022 Postoffice St., Galveston, TX 77550

There is a Roky Erickson lyric that perfectly describes the feeling you get when you walk into O'Malley's: "I have always been here before." This is about as close to the archetypical neighborhood sports bar as can be found in the Houston-Galveston area, from the classic American pub grub to the bric-a-brac for pro and college teams stuck all over the wall. O'Malley's is the type of place where you go to catch up with old friends you've just met.

POOP DECK
409-763-9151
2928? Seawall Blvd., Galveston, TX 77550

This a Galveston take on a Texas tradition, the icehouse. These venerable bars serve beer and lots of it in a relaxed atmosphere. The Poop Deck's visibility—it is located right on the seawall—plus its almost unforgettable slogan, "Where the elite meet and greet in their bare feet," have insured that this bar has become a favorite for the T-shirt and shorts crowd. It's a very friendly bar with a nice view of the Gulf.

21
409-762-2101
2102 Postoffice St. and 21st, Galveston, TX 77550

A mural on the seawall.

This upscale wine and martini bar offers 100 different wines, 50 by the glass, and 20 distinct martinis. Try the Aqua for a tropical feel (it's blue curaçao and vodka with a touch of pineapple juice and garnished with fresh pineapple). Or if you are in the mood for a salad, you could try the Taylor (vodka, very cold, garnished with pickled okra, baby corn, jal-o-beano, and olive). They also have live music five nights a week; the bands they book are generally more on the smooth R&B / down-tempo side. This isn't the place to rock out.

WHISKY'S ALL AMERICAN PUB
409-750-8497
2002 Postoffice St., Galveston, TX 77550

This was voted best bar in Galveston 2005 and 2006. Whisky's is definitely a place to go if you want to listen to some great origi-nal rock music played by up-and-coming bands, most of them from the Houston-Galveston area. The drinks are reasonably priced, and the bar has daily specials that make it even more affordable. You might be able to say that you saw the next Los Lonely Boys, who were one of the first acts to play Whisky's, back when they were playing bars for $8 cover charges.

YAGA'S CAFE AND BAR
409-762-6676
2314 Strand, Galveston, TX 77550

This touristy live-music venue on the Strand, run by the Galveston Restaurant Group that sells Mario's/Papa's pizzas along with pricey drinks, definitely appeals to the tank-top, sandals, and shorts set. If you go here, expect to overhear conversations about football and cars.

ATTRACTIONS

Galveston has always been a pleasant place to spend a beautiful spring or fall day, with the sea breeze blowing in, and the cries of the gulls mingling with the sounds from the street musicians on the Strand. The problem is, most people think that there isn't much to do otherwise. Actually, there is quite a bit to do in Galveston, but like everything else here, finding it is the hard part. This is because no matter how much the Galveston Chamber of Commerce or board of tourism says you're welcome to come on down, the locals on the street are liable to think of you as not a BOI (born on the island) or an IBC (islander by choice). So, to save you the trouble of asking, here's a list of some of the more popular attractions and all the monthly events that occur in Galveston throughout the year.

THE BISHOP'S PALACE

409-762-2475
1402 Broadway, Galveston, TX 77550

This ornate example of Victorian architecture harks back to a time when Galveston truly was a thriving port. Built in 1886 by Galveston attorney and congressional representative Colonel Walter Gresham and designed by Texas's premiere architect, Nicholas Clayton, the palace was constructed from native Texas granite, white limestone, and red sandstone, with all stones being cut and shaped on the premises. The hand-carved woodwork used many rare woods like rosewood, satinwood, and white mahogany. During the construction Colonel Gresham purchased fireplaces and mantels from around the world, had them imported to Galveston, and then had the rooms con-

The view from the balcony at the Bishop's Palace.

structed around them. The front ballroom mantel won first prize at the Philadelphia World's Fair in 1876, and the music room's mantel and fireplace are lined with pure silver. In 1923 the Galveston-Houston Diocese purchased the home for Bishop Christopher Byrne, who lived here until his death in 1950.

GALVESTON RAILROAD MUSEUM

409-765-5700
www.galvestonmuseum.com
123 Rosenberg (25th St. and the Strand), Galveston, TX 77550

Housed in one of the most eye-catching buildings on Galveston Island, this museum charts the history of Texas rail from its inception in 1836 to the present. The museum has a permanent collection of 41 different railroad cars, from steam engines to cabooses and everything in between. They also have the largest collection of railroad china in the United States. One of the nobler things about this museum is that while its primary focus is on preserving the history of rail in Texas, it is also one of the leading advocates for the establishment of a commuter rail line between the central business district of Houston and Galveston.

THE GRAND 1894 OPERA HOUSE

409-765-1894 or 1-800-821-1894
www.thegrand.com
2020 Postoffice St., Galveston, TX 77550

Designated by the 73rd Texas Legislature as the "Official Opera House of the State of Texas," the Grand has hosted some of the best and brightest performers of every generation, and not just opera singers. In the early years it hosted such international stars as Ignacz Paderewski and Anna Pavlova, and subsequently has seen such luminaries as Bill Cosby, Gregory Hines, Tim Conway, Willie Nelson, Harvey Korman, and Paul Anka, along with musicals

like *Cabaret* and *Rent*. With a season featuring more than 28 productions and 70 shows by visiting artists, including Broadway musicals, dance, drama, opera, and stars of the stage and screen, the Grand is one of the cultural bastions of Galveston Island. It is also an example of classic Victorian architecture, with staggered three-tier balconies, hand-carved scrollwork, and mosaic inlays. Anyone attending a performance should arrive early and treat themselves to a self-guided tour.

LONE STAR FLIGHT MUSEUM

409-740-7702 or 1-888-354-4488
www.lonestarflight.org
2002 Terminal Dr., Galveston, TX 77550

Home to the premiere flying collection of historic aircraft in the state of Texas, the Lone Star Flight Museum is one of Galveston's more awe-inspiring museums. Its 100,000-square-foot facility houses many examples of famous planes, including the B-17 Flying Fortress *Thunderbird*, which returned from 116 bombing missions over occupied Europe in World War II, and one of the only still-flying PBY Catalinas in the world.

MOODY GARDENS

800-582-4673 or 1-800-582-4673
www.moodygardens.com
One Hope Blvd., Galveston, TX 77550

If Disney World ran a natural science museum it would be like Moody Gardens. Technically Moody Gardens is a 501(c) (3) educational destination that uses nature to advance rehabilitation, conservation, recreation, and research, but for a nonprofit they sure make people pay a lot. Almost everything on this 242-acre resort destination requires the purchase of a separate ticket. Unless money is no object, be wary about taking children here. On the plus side, it does offer a chance to see many different types of animals and plants up close and personal, thanks to the Rain-forest and Aquarium Pyramids and cruise on the *Colonel*, an authentic 1840s paddle wheeler. The day cruises provide an interesting tour of Galveston's harbor, with narration about the history of Galveston, the Moody family, and Moody Gardens, while the evening cruise offers dinner, drinks, and dancing as the sun sets.

SCHLITTERBAHN WATERPARK

409-770-9283
www.schlitterbahn.com
2026 Lockheed Dr., Galveston, TX 77550

This heated, climate-controlled water park is the newest member of the largest water park chain in Texas. They have venues in New Braunfels, South Padre Island, and

The Sacred Heart Church of Galveston.

now Galveston. Since this location hasn't even been open a year, it's impossible to say how it will fare. It may be in for an uphill struggle with the locals, whose constant refrain is, "Why come to the beach to go to a water park?" But if any company can overcome such resistance, it would be Schlitterbahn. Their flagship location in New Braunfels has been voted the best water park in the world for nine consecutive years by *Amusement Today* magazine. It'll be interesting to see what they do with their new Galveston location, which does serve alcohol, by the way.

The Ocean Star *oil rig, now deactivated, serves as a museum for the history of deepwater oil exploration.*

STRAND THEATRE
409-763-4591
www.strandtheatregalveston.org
2317 Mechanic St., Galveston, TX 77550

Starting in 1977 the Strand Street Theatre began producing plays on Galveston Island. The next year they filed to become a not-for-profit corporation and moved into the 1897 Oppenheimer Building in the then newly revitalized Strand historic district. They've since become one of the crown jewels of the island's cultural scene. They do have a fairly short season, only approximately four shows a year, with an average run of about three weeks per show. Unlike many theaters that cast only from within their own company, the Strand holds public auditions.

TEXAS SEAPORT MUSEUM / ELISSA
409-763-1877
www.tsm-elissa.org
Pier 21, Galveston, TX 77550

Built in 1877, the three-masted tall ship *Elissa* has been designated an American treasure. Before she was rescued from a salvage yard, the *Elissa*, an iron-hulled bark, had been used by a Greek shipping company to haul cargo. After a $4.2 million restoration, the *Elissa* has become a window into the great age of sail. The Texas

Seaport Museum, where she is berthed, offers a brief introduction to the history of Galveston as a port and immigration depot. It also has an immigration database with information about more than 133,000 immigrants who entered the U.S. through Galveston. Pier 21 is also home to the Pier 21 Theatre, which shows documentaries on the Great Storm and the Gulf Coast's most famous pirate, Jean Laffite, who is rumored to have buried treasure all over Galveston Island.

EVENTS

ARTWALK
Every six weeks starting January 21

This open-studio tour showcases many of Galveston's best galleries, antiques shops, clothing stores, and boutiques, all with free wine.

MARDI GRAS
February; dates vary yearly

While the Galveston version of this traditional holiday is not as famous as its Louisiana cousin, with 9 parades and 15 masquerade balls it is no less eventful. There are three live music stages and plenty of beads to go around, although not as much drinking and topless women.

FEATHER FEST
March 30–April 2

This event kicks off the beginning of the spring migration of songbirds, which lasts until early May. Over the four-day celebration, members of the Audubon Society teach birding classes and conduct tours throughout the Galveston area. At the end of each day there is a cocktail social hour for participants.

KAPPA BEACH PARTY
Last weekend in April

What started as a fraternity spring break party has become one of the largest beach parties in the United States. This celebration of all things African American annually draws more than 35,000 people and some of the biggest names in hip-hop, soul, and R&B for what inevitably becomes a great festival. Aside from music, partying, and hooking up, Kappa weekend also offers one of the largest free custom car shows in the state. Of course, the vast amount of black people descending on the island for three solid days irks some white Galvestonians to no end. You can expect to see extra police, some stores closed down, and maybe even speed traps along I-45.

CINCO DE MAYO
May 5

Sponsored by the League of United Latin American Citizens (LULAC), the Fiesta de la Isla (Festival of the Island) commemorates Mexico's independence from Spain with a fajita cook off, mariachi contest, parade, and outdoor concert.

AMERICAN INSTITUTE OF ARCHITECTS SANDCASTLE COMPETITION
June 3

This is truly a visual feast as architects, engineers, and designers strive to create their best sand creation in an effort to raise funds for the Houston chapter of the AIA. Entries are judged on artistic execution, technical difficulty, carving technique, and originality.

WINGS OVER HOUSTON AIRSHOW
First weekend of October

This is great place to take kids and military airplane buffs. They get to see current and retired military aircraft, stunt craft, the Blue Angels, and all sorts of other incredible things.

OKTOBERFEST
Last weekend of October

The traditional German festival featuring *Wurst und Bier*. There is plenty of fun for those who don't drink, with German "oompah" music, dancing, a live auction, raffle, and tours.

LONE STAR MOTORCYCLE RALLY
First weekend of November

Sponsored by the Galveston Park Board, this four-day island-wide celebration draws over 250,000 bikers and motorcycle enthusiasts. The largest biker rally in the state of Texas, it features motorcycle processions, beach drag races, Lil' Hawg races, live music, poker runs, custom bike contests, and concept vehicle shows. Because of Galveston's proximity, it is a very popular weekend destination for the Houston area's biker community. It is not uncommon to be walking the streets of Galveston and see people in full biker colors.

DICKENS ON THE STRAND
First weekend in December

Every December the Strand is turned into Victorian England, complete with the Queen Victoria herself. Many local artisans and craftspeople ply their wares, and those with a good eye can spot some familiar characters strolling the streets. Dickens on the Strand is the third-largest Christmas celebration in the United States, attracting some 125,000 visitors for its Friday-night-through-Sunday-afternoon activities. It features a parade complete with bagpipers and an appearance by Her Majesty.

SPORTS AND RECREATION

GALVESTON COLLEGE WHITECAPS
409-944-4242
www.gc.edu
4015 Avenue Q, Galveston, TX 77550

There are only three sports in the Galveston College athletics department: baseball, softball, and volleyball. The relative smallness of the department, and the lack of any television interest, helps to keep the sports honest and down-to-earth. Sure, they give athletic scholarships, but they go to kids from places like Little Axe, Oklahoma. It's definitely worth stopping in to watch a game—especially when the fog rolls in and covers the baseball diamond and you can't see the second baseman from the bleachers and you wonder how in the world these kids are playing in conditions like this.

GULF GREYHOUND PARK
409-986-9500
www.gulfgreyhound.com
I-45 South, exit 15
(15 miles north of Galveston in La Marque)

This 110-acre, 6,600-seat, three-level arena is boasted to be the largest dog track

Just off the Strand you can't miss the Galveston Square Trumpe, one of the most famous of all public art projects in Texas.

in the world. It has 318 teller windows, the parking lot can accommodate 8,000 vehicles, and the entire track can hold 14,000 people. The track offers more than a dozen ways to bet, with "betting buddies" available on every floor to explain how to place a wager and answer any questions. The races—or performances, as the management likes to call them—are held every week, Wednesday through Sunday. Times vary day to day, so check before attending.

Golf

GALVESTON ISLAND MUNICIPAL GOLF COURSE
1700 Sydnor Lane
Galveston, TX 77554
409-741-4626

This course, just beyond Scholes airport and only 5 miles from downtown, was reworked in 1991 by Carlton Gipson, who designed some of the Houston area's best courses. Gipson took the preexisting course and tweaked it to take advantage of the location along Sydnor Bayou, which brings water hazards into play on 14 of 18 holes. Beware the par threes; two are almost all water.

GALVESTON COUNTRY CLUB
14228 Stewart Rd.
Galveston, TX 77554
409-737-9800

This was the first chartered country club in Texas and the first course to be designed by a professional golf course architect. It claims to be the oldest country club in continuous operation. It's been around for 110 years and has seen hurricanes, hard times, and heroics. And to top it all off it's a good course, too. It's adjacent to Galveston Island State Park.

SHOPPING AND SERVICES

There are two main shopping areas in Galveston: the Strand and the seawall. The Strand offers a slightly more varied mix of shops, restaurants, and bars than the seawall.

BARGAIN BEACHWEAR
409-762-6334
4708 Seawall Blvd., Galveston, TX 77550

This *turista* shop caters to beachgoers, and the selection of T-shirts, hats, swimwear, and so on is fairly predictable. It's the type of place where girls can get swimsuits that look like beer bottle labels and guys can get T-shirts with pick-up lines screen-printed on them—in short, a place popular with the spring break crowd, as well as those who think that every time they go to the beach it is spring break.

BATH JUNKIE
409-766-1959
2029 Strand, Galveston, TX 77550

This high-end bath and body product store, with locations throughout the South, describes itself as "a deli for bath stuff." They create custom fragrances from more than 150 different bases and can make any fragrance in any color.

CHIMERA'S DEN
409-740-1589
6018 Stewart Rd., Galveston, TX 77550

One of the only comics and games stores in Galveston, Chimera's is out on the west side of the island and has a fairly limited selection.

GALVESTON BOOKSHOP
409-750-8200 or 877-750-8200
317 23rd St. (between Strand and Mechanic) Galveston, TX 77550

This is Galveston's only used bookstore. Their stock, like that of any used bookstore, fluctuates depending on what they have purchased, but there's always the chance that some true gems can be found. A plus is the chairs scattered throughout the store, so that you can peruse that out-of-print curiosity in comfort.

HAVA CIGAR
409-621-1166
2107 Seawall Blvd.
(21st at the beach, at the Balinese),
Galveston, TX 77550

Located in the 600-foot Balinese Room breezeway, this is Galveston's premiere cigar shop. With a large selection of premium cigars and accessories, this is a fantastic place to sip on a nice cocktail from the Balinese, puff on a Montecristo, and watch behind the island while listening to the crash of the waves on the beach.

HENDLEY MARKET
800-349-8375
2010 Strand, Galveston, TX 77550

This somewhat pricey gift shop happens to be one of the few places on the Strand where you can find things other than T-shirts with sophomoric slogans, flip-flops, and pseudo surfer wear. They carry a large selection of goods imported from Asia and Latin America, as well as many antique books, Dover Thrift Editions, and some of the classics of world literature. It is definitely worth stopping by, if only to see the vintage freak-show banners hanging on the walls.

INHAIRITANCE SALON
409-762-6640
523 24th St., Suite 201
(24th and Postoffice Sts.), Galveston, TX 77550

This is one of the only salons on Galveston Island that offers complete hair and nail care as well as a fully qualified massage therapist on site. It might just be the thing to help you relax and get ready for a day at the beach. They do welcome walk-ins.

LA KING'S CONFECTIONERY
409-762-6100
www.lakingscandy.com
E-mail: lakings@eazylink.com
2323 Strand, Galveston, TX 77550

La King's is a rarity. Not only is it one of the few candy makers in Texas that has stayed family owned and operated for more than 80 years; it's also one of the very few with a store and possibly the only one that uses traditional recipes, traditional equipment, and has an authentic soda fountain serving authentic fountain delights. One does not truly understand the nature of the milkshake until one has one made on an authentic 1920s blender.

MAMADY PRIMITIVE ART DEALER
409-763-5855
2211 Strand, Galveston, TX 77550

While the concept of a store selling primitive art from Africa isn't new or original, Mamady does it in such a way that it seems new and original. Another of the things that separates Mamady from similar stores elsewhere is its lower prices. So if you have always wanted some authentic Sudanese art or a guitar from Ghana but could never afford it, this is the place for you. Shoe-horned in among the tacky tourist shops of the Strand and the endless antiques stores of Galveston, Mamady is surprisingly refreshing. Let's hope it lasts.

Workers cope with a Sunday afternoon rush at La King's.

A resident of Galveston takes in the sights along the Strand.

THE MARKET
409-621-2007
2510 Market St. (between 25th and 26th Sts.; 2 blocks off Strand), Galveston, TX 77550

This two-and-a-half-story gem of an antiques store sells everything in working condition. Sadly, that luxury is costly; almost everything seems to be well past the $100 mark. However, some rarities are worth the price.

MIDSUMMER BOOKS
409-765-5930
2311 Mechanic St. at 23rd (1 block off Strand), Galveston, TX 77550

This is a nice, quiet, independently owned bookstore with stacks that tend to skew toward the most widely read and the most recent offerings from literary luminaries. The staff is knowledgeable and well-read and isn't afraid to engage in discussion and offer recommendations. The store also has a fairly active role in promoting authors, so it is just possible that there might be a reading or talk scheduled when you're around.

OHANA SURF & SKATE
409-763-2700
28th St. and Seawall Blvd., Galveston, TX 77550

This is one of Galveston's many surf shops; it holds three-day beginner's surfing workshops throughout the summer and offers a large selection of surfing accessories. It also carries a wide range of surfboards from local and national companies.

OLD THYMER'S HERBS
409-762-8836
4607 Avenue R?, Galveston, TX 77550

This is Galveston's only herb shop. They carry the basics and a little bit more.

PEANUT BUTTER WAREHOUSE
409-762-8358
www.peanutbutterwarehouse.com
102 20th St. (between the Strand and Harborside Dr.), Galveston, TX 77550

Built in 1895, this three-story warehouse was used to store candy and peanut butter until the Great Storm shifted the import business elsewhere. Its 25,000 square feet are now used to display antiques and collectibles from 25 different merchants. This is the only place on the island where it is possible to find issues of *Life* magazine from 1947, sword canes, freshly ground peanut butter, and gourmet coffee all in the same location. The prices are fairly reasonable, and many of the items make great gifts for the person with eclectic taste. After all, who wouldn't want a spyglass with tripod or vintage World War II—era advertisements?

DAY TRIPS

While Galveston can be a fascinating place to explore, it can wear you down. Fortunately, what's outside Galveston can be just as fascinating, if not more. What is wonderful about the areas around Galveston is how radically different they are. They range from full-blown Houston suburbs with immaculate lawns and gated communities to the surreal, alien cityscape of massive petrochemical plants, with down-and-out fishing villages and hard-luck industrial towns thrown into the mix for good measure. This buffet of disparate ingredients that makes up the American cultural landscape can be sampled from your car window on a simple drive to the beach.

Clear Lake Area

The area north of Galveston is geographically defined by Galveston Bay. However, it is culturally defined by the proximity to NASA's Johnson Space Center and the petrochemical industry. These two things have made this part of Texas one of the more solidly upper middle class areas in the state, with the median household income easily falling into the $100K+ a year range. The two most notorious of these Houston exurbs are Kemah and Seabrook.

Seabrook

(From Galveston: Take I-45 north to NASA Road 1.) Located just up TX 146 from Kemah, Seabrook is a bedroom community that depends on the Johnson Space Center as its primary industry. The main reason why Seabrook is so well-known is the incessant radio advertising of the Seabrook Beach Club. This bar, the joke goes, is larger than some Latin American countries and features more TVs than most. If there is such a thing as a Disneyland for twenty-somethings, this might qualify. It has 20 TVs, a full-size swimming pool, swim-up bar, volleyball net, pool table, live music, karaoke, full-service kitchen, and thatched roof *palapas* that offer a great view of Clear Lake. If they added a hot tub and their own hotel, they might become a great spring-break destination.

Once you get past the tourist trap of SBC, you can find some good-quality brew pubs and a few good restaurants, most of which are populated by recent college grads who are working for NASA. Think more along the lines of data processors than astronauts.

Local residents make their way to a waiting ship.

Freeport to Angleton Area

This mini-sprawl encompasses eight towns and was built with petrodollars; the residents live in Dow Chemical's shadow. The Freeport petrochemical facility spans over 10 miles, making it one of the largest in the state. Just driving the edge of the refinery takes a good 15 to 20 minutes. The Dow plant is a city within a city, with its own fire and police departments, its own barge canal, and two major highways running through it. It's also the largest employer in the county.

An oil rig waits to go to sea, a common occurrence on the Texas coast.

Surfside

(From Galveston: Take San Luis Pass Road, FM 3005, over the San Luis Pass Bridge. Once you cross the bridge FM 3005 becomes FM 257, which is also known as Blue Water Highway. Keep going.) Driving down San Luis Pass Road to Surfside from Galveston takes you past Bastrop Bay—named for a Dutchman who impersonated the Baron de Bastrop to help Stephen F. Austin's first group of colonists secure the right to settle, in 1822, then Christmas Bay, so-called because the Austin colonists saw it on Christmas day—and through the Brazoria National Wildlife Refuge. When you arrive at the somewhat isolated fishing village of Surfside, the first thing you notice is the air of semipermanence. It seems like all the A-frame stilt houses could blow away with the next good wind. Don't worry, though—many of them have been there for 30 or more years. One in particular, the Octagon, has been there so long it's a landmark for local surfers. This is because by lining up directly in front of the building it was possible to catch a wave and get a good 5- to 10-minute ride out of it; sadly, the erosion of the beaches has made a ride like that almost impossible. Across the jetty from Surfside is Quintana, which has a unique place in Texas history. This is where Austin and his colonists landed in 1822.

Freeport

(From Galveston: Take San Luis Pass Rd., aka FM 3005, over the San Luis Bridge. It then becomes FM 257, aka BlueWater Highway. When 257 connects with State Highway 332 in Surfside take a right. Stay on 332 until it hits FM 523 and take a left.) To some people this is a perfect example of life on coastal Texas; to others it's a boring small town. Freeport has 45 restaurants, 10 bars, one golf course, a state park, a county park, a municipal park, and 3.9 miles of fairly unspoiled beach. The beaches are the primary reason people come here. There's no real live music scene, and nothing much goes on except fishing, surfing, and drinking. It does have Wal-Mart, though.

Lake Jackson

(From Galveston: Take San Luis Pass Rd., aka FM 3005, over the San Luis Bridge. It then becomes FM 257, aka BlueWater Highway. When 257 connects with TX 332 in Surfside take a right. Stay on 332 until it connects with 288, which should be right outside Clute, then veer to the left, which should put you on 288 headed north.) Even though this is the largest city in the area, Lake Jackson is still pretty much like any standard exurban small town in the U.S. It's filled with the typical chain restaurants you'll find elsewhere. It does have both a municipal golf course and country club, though.

Angleton

(From Lake Jackson: Stay on 288 past the airport and take a right on 35, aka West Mulberry Street.) This small industrial town of approximately 19,000 people is growing at a rate of 3.5 percent per year. It's a middle-class, blue-collar town filled with young people. The average income is $43,000 a year, with the majority of men working construction or at the chemical plant and the majority of women working in education or health care. It's known as a place that has a deep love of high school football and the outdoors and is filled with people who aren't afraid to say "howdy" and "y'all." It's a quiet place, with a town motto of "Where the heart is."

A public art piece on the Texas coast.

Texas City Area

(From Galveston: Take I-45 north to the Texas City junction. Exit onto TX 146, aka TX 3, aka Old Galveston Highway. Stay on 146.) Texas City is one of the largest cities in Galveston County. It boasts the world's longest man-made fishing pier, the Texas City Dike, the second-largest petroleum plant in the U.S. (the BP plant), and a history that includes the worst industrial accident in the U.S. That occurred in 1947 when a cargo ship full of ammonium nitrate and ammunition blew up at approximately 8 AM and killed 581 people and injured 5,000. The explosion was so large that it was mistaken for the detonation of an atomic bomb. The injuries, loss of life, destruction of property, and other general carnage that were caused by the explosion led to the first class-action lawsuit against the U.S. government. Initially a district court found the U.S. government and 168 different agencies and their representatives guilty of various negligent acts in the manufacture, packaging, and labeling of ammonium nitrate. However, the U.S. government appealed, and the decision was reversed by a higher court, which found that the U.S. government had the right to exercise its discretion in matters vital to national security. The residents of Texas City appealed to the U.S. Supreme Court and lost.

The Road between Galveston and Corpus Christi

If you truly want to gain an understanding of Texas, you have to drive it. From Galveston to Corpus Christi alone is approximately 200 miles, a distance that normally takes two and a half to three hours. While that is a lot of driving, in most Texans' eyes it's a normal amount to drive in a day. If you decide to see the state through the windshield, there are a few places of note along the way:

West Columbia

Located west of Angleton on TX 35, this small, out-of-the-way town can take some driving to get to, and the trip probably should be made only by the true Texas history / historical home devotees. The main destinations here are the Columbia Historical Museum, which has an exhibit on the history of East Columbia (a thriving port when steamships plied the Brazos River), and the Varner-Hogg Plantation. The plantation's main house is a Greek-revival-style mansion; it was built in the 1830s by the state of Texas's first rum distiller. It changed hands many times, finally owned by James Stephen Hogg, Texas's first native-born governor.

Palacios

Located on Texas Highway 35, this sleepy town holds a special place in U.S. civil rights history. It was the centerpiece of a historic legal battle that broke the Ku Klux Klan. In April 1981 the Vietnamese Fishermen's Association and the Southern Poverty Law Center filed suit against United Klans of America Inc.—who were headquartered at the time off Redbluff Road in Pasadena, Texas, an exurb of Houston. The suit charged UKA with unfair practices against economic competitors, harassment, and a myriad of other offenses that stemmed from the Klan's campaign of intimidation against Vietnamese shrimpers. The campaign was marked with fiery rhetoric, dozens of burned shrimp boats, and a Klan gunboat patrolling the coast. In Palacios the most heated battleground was a trailer park that the Klan surrounded and the Vietnamese barricaded themselves into. Sadly, none of

Looking inland from the Texas City Dike.

A woman tries her luck fishing in a culvert.

this was new; the Klan had been doing the same thing to one ethnic minority or another for generations, with criminal charges rarely being filed for a variety of reasons—corruption, fear, racism, etc. What made this case unique was that the attorney, Morris Dees, realized that the Vietnamese wouldn't win a criminal case, but they could win a civil one. The case came to Judge Gabriel Kirk McDonald—Texas's first African American federal judge—in May of 1981. McDonald ruled against the Klan, ordering them to cease their coastal activities, disband any armed groups, give up their paramilitary training camps, and make restitution for any damage done. The case made national news, inspired a documentary called *Alamo Bay*, and utterly destroyed the largest Klan group in the nation. The judgment was so large that 30 years later the Klan still hasn't been able to pay it off. The only other thing of note in Palacios is the Luther Hotel. The Luther was built in 1903 and is the only Texas coast resort hotel still standing. At the turn of the 20th century hotels like the Luther were fairly common, "grand ladies" built in a southern style, with large porches and opulent rooms. Sadly, as the world moved on they were overlooked and neglected. This hotel has been restored to its former glory and is definitely worth staying at.

LUTHER HOTEL
361-972-2312
409 S. Bay Blvd., Palacios, TX 77465
Price: Inexpensive to Moderate
Credit Cards: V, MC

Innkeepers Dolly and Billy Hamlin have made this one of the best deals on the Texas coast. For what it would cost to stay one night at a fancier, more modern hotel, you can stay a whole week here. It's rumored that a young Frank Sinatra stayed in the penthouse, which you can get for a song. If you are staying in Palacios, this is the place to be.

Port Lavaca

Across Matagorda Bay from Palacios is the slightly bigger town of Port Lavaca. Although this place is primarily known for its fishing pier, it does have other offerings. It is home to the Calhoun County Museum, which has a scale model of the town of Indianola before it was destroyed by a hurricane, and the original lens of the Halfmoon Reef Lighthouse. It has the Halfmoon Reef Lighthouse, too, which was relocated in 1979 from Matagorda Bay to the Highway 35 bypass. The lighthouse was built in 1858 and stayed operational until the 1940s. Port Lavaca is also home to the Indianola State Historic Site. This commemorative park details the history of one of the most famous ghost towns in Texas. Indianola was the main point of entry for colonists immigrating into the Republic of Texas in the 1840s; it was where the U.S. Camel Corps landed in 1852; it was blockaded and shelled by the Union in the Civil War before Confederate forces spiked their guns and retreated to the mainland; it suffered through a yellow fever epidemic, a horrible hurricane in 1866, another in 1875, and was finally destroyed by a third direct hit in 1886. The park also has a statue of the French explorer La Salle, who landed on Matagorda Island in 1685. For bird lovers and naturalists, this is a premiere spot. During the spring migration more than four hundred species of birds descend on Port Lavaca. Some stay for only a few days, but others hang around for weeks.

CALHOUN COUNTY MUSEUM

361-553-4689
www.calhouncountymuseum.org
301 S. Ann St., Port Lavaca, TX 77979

This museum is dedicated to preserving the history and culture of Calhoun County; it has artifacts from the prehistoric settlement of the area and from the 1686 wreck of the *Belle*, La Salle's ship. Exhibits document the power struggle that resulted from La Salle's intrusion into what was then Spanish territory, German immigration into Texas in the mid to late 1800s, Civil War battles that took place in Calhoun County, and the destruction of the town of Indianola. This is a must-see for the true Texas history buff.

HALFMOON REEF LIGHTHOUSE

TX 35

This beautiful octagonal wooden structure is not exactly what people think of when they hear the word "lighthouse." It's not very tall, just a few stories. It isn't very remote—it's right off the freeway now. However, during the spring migration, this is considered to be one of the premiere places to see warblers in the United States.

INDIANOLA STATE HISTORIC SITE

The end of TX 316 at Indianola Beach

This site details and commemorates the now-vanished town of Indianola and the almost forgotten Civil War battle fought here in an attempt to keep Matagorda Bay out of the hands of Union forces.

A gracious historic home on the Texas coast.

CORPUS CHRISTI

Crescent Moon of the Coastal Bend

In 1519, on the Feast of Corpus Christi, Alonso Álvarez de Pineda was sailing along the Texas coast when he discovered what he described as "a beautiful bay." In a moment of religious and poetic brilliance Pineda named the bay "Corpus Christi," Latin for "body of Christ." For the next three hundred years Corpus Christi Bay was relatively unused. However, three years after the Texas War for Independence, in 1839, a frontier trading post was established on the shores of the bay. The post was built near what is now the 400 block of Broadway, and soon after the establishment of this trading post—a post that, unlike most other frontier settlements, could be supplied by ship—people started to come. They arrived so slowly at first—a dozen here, twenty there—that it seemed like Corpus (as it's now often called by Texans) was destined to be just a frontier outpost. And then Texas joined the United States. The importance of this for the city of Corpus Christi can't be understated, because when Texas joined the union, the U.S. government became involved in a border dispute with Mexico and dispatched General Zachary Taylor and an expeditionary force to Corpus Christi. As the diplomats in Washington and Mexico City talked, Taylor and his men arrived in Corpus and established what can only be called a tent city. They also brought law and order with them (before their arrival, Corpus didn't even have a cemetery). Finally the diplomats had nothing else to say, and the U.S. went to war with Mexico. Taylor and his men headed south, but it wasn't long before more soldiers came and took their place. By this time Corpus Christi Bay had become an important link in the supply chain for the Mexican War. During the Civil War Corpus was blockaded by Union forces but because of its distance from the front lines was fairly unimportant. After the war, it continued to be the drop-off point for operations in the West—Indian wars, border disputes, and the pursuit of Emiliano Zapata were all supplied through Corpus.

As the 19th century gave way to the 20th, life in Corpus didn't change much, until the U.S. government decided in the 1920s to make Corpus a deepwater port. This decision more than anything else changed Corpus forever. After the Corps of Engineers dredged the bay to make it the deepest place on the Texas coast, the population exploded and the town expanded.

Corpus is a now a picturesque city of approximately 300,000. Like most cities it is a mixture of impressions and ideas. Known by some as the birthplace of both Eva Longoria and Selena, among Texas musicians Corpus is known for a near

Definition
Coastal Bend: A reference to the mid-area of the Texas Coast "where it bends south and heads toward Mexico."

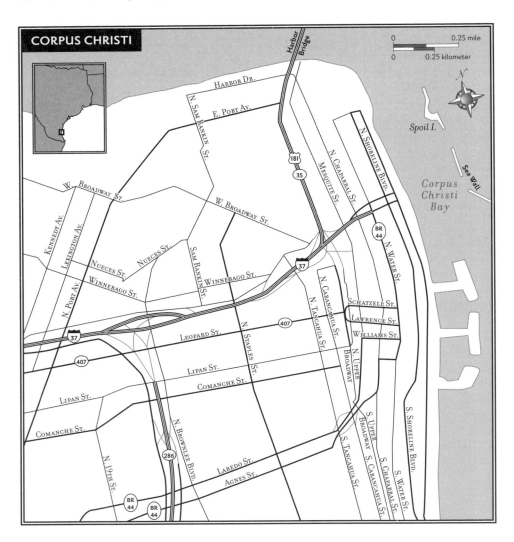

legendary hardcore punk/metal scene. In surfing circles it is home to the famous Bob Hall Pier Surfing contest. For high school thespians all over the state, Corpus is known as one of the homes of the annual Texas Thespian convention. And for thousands of people, Corpus is known as home to a Naval Air Station, which is part of the Navy's jet training program. The tourism industry knows Corpus as "the shining city by the sea." I will always think of Corpus as "the place where I threw a drive belt and had to walk 5 miles to find a Wal-Mart." Admittedly it was a walk through beautiful neighborhoods, filled with historic homes and nice people in gorgeous weather.

GETTING TO CORPUS

By Air

If you aren't like me and don't want to risk breaking down just outside town and having to walk, you might want to fly. Fortunately, that is possible.

Corpus Christi International Airport: 361-289-0171; www.corpuschristiairport.com; 1000 International Blvd. (corner of Agnes St. and Joe Mireur Rd.), Corpus Christi, TX 78406

This is essentially a commuter airport and is served by small carriers, such as Expressjet, or the commuter wings of big carriers, like Continental Express. The majority of the flights are to and from destinations in and around Texas; this means that you will most likely have to catch a connection in Dallas or Houston. Flights generally are scheduled only during business hours, about 8 to 6. However, the airport is conveniently near town, which makes getting around very easy after you arrive. If you are flying to Corpus via private plane, you might want to consider filing a flight plan for the smaller municipal airport.

Nueces County Airport: 3983 Wings Dr., Robstown, TX 78380

Since this is a small airfield with no regular service, housing a private plane is not that difficult.

By Car

If you are like me and don't mind driving across the vast stretches of nothingness that make up Texas, you'll need directions.

From Houston: Take US 59 south past Victoria and Beeville until you hit I-37. I-37 south will take you straight to Corpus.

From San Antonio: Head south on I-37.

By Bus or Train

If you are a romantic with visions of touring the Texas countryside from the observation car of a train, I'm sorry. Amtrak doesn't run to Corpus. In fact, Corpus Christi hasn't had a passenger service or rail-based mass transit system for decades. However, there is a proposal for the Corpus Christi Regional Transportation Authority to get into the light rail business. We'll see whether or not it happens. As for bus links, while Corpus Christi has two Greyhound stops, the frequency of the bus stopping is very unpredictable. So please call for availability, prices, and schedule before attempting. The two Greyhound stops are:

Corpus Christi VTC Station: 702 N. Chaparral St., Corpus Christi, TX 78401; 361-882-2516 or 1-800-231-222

Stripes Store Exxon: 11201 IH 37, Corpus Christi, TX 78410; 361-242-3456 or 1-800-231-2222

By Boat

Sadly, there are no cruise lines operating in Corpus Christi as of this writing, although the Port of Corpus Christi and the city of San Antonio have teamed up to try to lure one. They

A slip at the marina.

built a nice new terminal and are pushing to get someone to use Corpus as a home port. However, if you have your own boat, this is where Corpus Christi really comes into its own. Nowhere else in Texas has a better bay than Corpus, and the pride of that bay is the municipal marina.

Corpus Christi Marina: 361-826-3980; www.corpuschristimarina.com; 400 Lawrence St., Corpus Christi, 78401

Corpus has one of the most beautiful marinas in the state of Texas, and if you are planning on yachting on the Texas coast, Corpus is the place to do it. Nothing could be finer than to launch at Galveston and take a cabin cruiser down to Corpus and South Padre Island. Mooring at Corpus isn't terribly expensive—approximately $27 a night, or 90 cents per foot.

Getting Around Corpus

Corpus is one of the most beautiful cities in Texas and begs to be explored by any means necessary. The most obvious is from behind the wheel of a car. This is really not that hard to do, as Corpus is laid out fairly logically. It doesn't adhere to the grid formula like Galveston, but it also doesn't have six-way intersections where all the streets have the same name, like San Antonio. So driving around isn't much of a problem. In fact, most of the city of Corpus Christi is within 15 miles of the coast.

Car Rentals

If you flew down and want to rent a car, Corpus has plenty of places to rent from. All the major national chains have a presence here, and most have offices at the airport. I have listed only one location for each agency here, despite the fact that almost all have multiple locations. A selection of the most well-known agencies follows.

Advantage: 361-853-2277; 2727 N. Padre Island Dr., Corpus Christi, TX 78415

Avis Truck Rental: 361-289-0073; 1000 International Dr., Corpus Christi, TX 78469

Budget Rent A Car: 361-855-0656; 2902 South Padre Island Dr., Corpus Christi, TX 78415

Dollar Rent A Car: 1-866-434-2226; 1000 International Blvd., Corpus Christi, TX 78406

Enterprise Rent-A-Car: 361-884-7368; 823 N. Water St., Corpus Christi, TX 78401

Thrifty Car Rental: 361-289-0042; 1928 N. Padre Island Dr., Corpus Christi, TX 78408

Bicycles

Corpus has one of the best hike-and-bike trail networks in the state and has a relatively small square mileage. So it is very possible to see the majority of Corpus on bike. If you didn't think to bring yours with you, don't worry. Many hotels offer bike rental.

Public/Mass Transit

Sadly, Corpus doesn't have a Yellow Bike program, nor does it have a light rail system. This means that if you want to use mass transit in Corpus, you have to take the bus. The Corpus Christi Regional Transit Authority makes taking the bus complicated; they have 18 different day fares, ranging in price from free for children under five and seniors/disabled/Medicare transfers, to $3 for harbor ferry B-Line service. They also have nine different types of bus passes, ranging in price from $1.75 for a Day Run Pass to $50 for a B-Line Pass. The B-Line is curb-to-curb transportation for the disabled. Excluding B-Line service, which requires 24-hour notification for pickup, Corpus Christi Regional Transit Authority runs 28 separate bus routes through the city. Like anywhere else, riding the bus in Corpus requires lots of planning, and the buses stop running at 11 PM. For all the information on what bus lines run where and when, go to www.ccrta.org.

LODGING

It is worth repeating that prices change depending on the season. In some cases they double from their off-season levels. So it is best to call ahead and find out what to expect, especially since most hotels have cancellation fees. The hospitality industry in Corpus Christi is dominated by big-name budget motels, which is fine unless you want to be pampered; then your choices are fewer. The hotels listed here are not an endorsement, just a representative sampling of what is available.

BAHIA MAR

361-949-2400 or 1-800-671-9207
15021 Windward Dr., Corpus Christi, TX 78418
Price: Moderate
Credit Cards: AE, D, DC, MC, V

This is one of the most popular and well-reviewed hotels in Corpus, and with good reason. The staff is friendly, courteous, and helpful. The hotel is also directly across the street from one of the most beautiful beaches in Texas, and it is not extremely pricey.

BAYFRONT INN

361-883-7271
www.bayfrontinncc.com
601 N. Shoreline Blvd., Corpus Christi, TX 78401
Price: Low
Credit Cards: AE, MC, V

This Ramada Inn concept budget motel sits right at the end of the People's Street T-Head, which is one of the more famous piers in Texas. It offers basic cable, coin laundry, and discounts for those feeling the need to pinch their pennies. Check the Web site for a 10 percent off coupon.

BEST WESTERN MARINA GRAND

361-883-5111 or 1-800-883-5119
300 N. Shoreline Blvd., Corpus Christi, TX 78401
Price: Inexpensive to Moderate
Credit Cards: AE, D, DC, MC, V

This is the sixth-most-popular hotel in Corpus. It's on the waterfront, so you can lie in your bed and look at the bay. It has recently undergone a major renovation and improved all its rooms.

There's something about a quiet street on a summer Sunday afternoon.

CHRISTY ESTATES SUITES

361-854-1091 or 1-800-6-SUITE-6
www.christyestatessuites.com
3942 Holly Rd., Corpus Christi, TX 78415
Price: Moderate
Credit Cards: AE, CB, D, DC, MC, V

This hotel deserves credit for being one of the only larger establishments on the Texas coast to have theme rooms. Besides offering rooms with such tempting names as "Lucifer's Lair," Christy Estates caters to the business traveler market with its corporate suites and the transitional housing market with its apartment-size military lodging suites, both of which have a kitchen with full utensils, couches, and all the amenities you'll need for a few days. It also offers discounts for extended stays.

CLARION HOTEL

361-883-6161
www.clarioninn.com
5224 Navigation Blvd., Corpus Christi, TX 78407
Price: Low
Credit Cards: AE, CB, D, DC, MC, V

Located in the industrial area, this hotel has a polite staff, a decent breakfast, and a reasonable price tag. This is the perfect place for the no-nonsense business traveler.

FAIRFIELD INN
361-985-8393
www.mariott.com
5217 Blanche Moore Dr., Corpus Christi,
TX 78411
Price: Inexpensive
Credit Cards: AE, D, MC, V

This economy hotel by Marriott is located 1
mile from the two biggest malls, 10 miles
from the Gulf of Mexico, and 11 from the
airport. It is perfectly suited to family
travelers and is very kid-friendly.

HAWTHORN SUITES
361-814-5600
www.hawthorn.com
1442 South Padre Island Dr., Corpus
Christi, TX 78416
Price: Inexpensive
Credit Cards: AE, CB, D, DC, MC, V

Catering to business travelers, this hotel
offers complimentary voice mail, dual
phone lines, high-speed Internet, valet
and coin-operated laundry. Plus it is one
of the few hotels in Corpus to accept the
Japanese Credit Bureau Card.

HOLIDAY INN EMERALD BEACH
361-883-5731
www.holidayinn.com
1102 S. Shoreline Blvd., Corpus Christi, TX
78401
Price: Moderate
Credit Cards: AE, D, DC, MC, V

This resort-style hotel offers package
plans, sauna, whirlpool, fishing, table
tennis, pool table, bicycles, playground,
exercise room, shuffleboard, wave runner,
and game room rental. They also have a
gift shop and valet laundry service. All for
a moderate price tag. This is definitely a
family-friendly destination and is perfect
for vacations and other getaways.

KNIGHTS INN—BY THE BEACH
361-883-4411
3615 Timmons Blvd., Corpus Christi, TX
78402
Price: Inexpensive
Credit Cards: AE, D, DC, MC, V

This three-story, 40-room motel is
straightforward and fairly minimal in its
amenities. It has a pool, shuffleboard, and
volleyball. It also has one one-bedroom
suite. One of its main attractions is the fact
that the price doesn't change with the
season, so it remains one of the most
affordable places to stay in Corpus.

OMNI HOTELS
361-887-1600
www.omnihotels.com
900 N. Shoreline Blvd., Corpus Christi, TX
78401
Price: Moderate to High
Credit Cards: AE, CB, D, DC, MC, V

Without a doubt Omni towers are the best
hotels in Corpus, with big rooms, lots of
amenities, indoor pools, and a combined
capacity of more than 800 rooms. This is
living. Personally, I find the Bayfront
tower to be a little more appealing, but
neither one is a bad night's stay. If you are
going to Corpus, you should spend the
night here at least once. The location is
smack-dab in the middle of everything,
and the staff is courteous, conscientious,
and above all knowledgeable. They also
have a fantastic restaurant and a nice pool.

QUALITY INN
361-883-7456
3202 E. Surfside Blvd., Corpus Christi, TX
78403
Price: Inexpensive
Credit Cards: AE, CB, D, DC, MC, VI

This two-story, 112-room hotel features
eight one-bedroom suites and whirlpool

bathtubs. It is a very low-key establishment—just the place to unwind after a day of sightseeing or hanging out at the beach.

Bed & Breakfasts

In Corpus there is no standard definition of a bed & breakfast. They can be $75-a-night spare rooms or mansions. It may take a little digging to find the one that is right for you, but the ones selected here are some of the most well-established, well-recognized, and well-known in the city limits. There are others in the surrounding small towns, but those will be dealt with later.

FORTUNA BAY BED AND BREAKFAST

361-949-7554
www.ccinternet.net/fortunabay
E-mail: fortunabay@msn.com
15405 Fortuna Bay Dr. #12, Corpus Christi, TX 78418
Price: Moderate to Expensive
Credit Cards: AE, D, MC, V

This spacious 11-room B&B—all rooms with private bath—has one of the best sunsets in the Corpus metro area. It is a 15-minute drive to all the major attractions. Guests of this lovely establishment get club privileges at the Padre Isles Country Club and access to one the nicest courtyards in South Texas. They also offer full spa treatment (body massages, seaweed wraps, the works).

GEORGE BLUCHER HOUSE BED & BREAKFAST

361-884-4884 or 1-866-884-4884
www.georgebluicherhouse.com
211 North Carrizo St., Corpus Christi, TX 78401
Price: Moderate
Credit Cards: AE, MC, V

This historic Victorian home has been converted into a six-room B&B. In addition to the elegant traditional decor, it also boasts one of the more picturesque locations in a group of establishments that all sport picturesque locations. It is literally across the street from a bird sanctuary and next door to a block of historically preserved buildings.

OCEAN HOUSE

361-882-9500
www.oceansuites.com
3275 Ocean Dr., Corpus Christi, TX 78404
Price: Moderate to Expensive
Credit Cards: AE, D, MC, V

This 8,000-square-foot mansion was built in 1935 and has been updated and remodeled. It now has a 1-acre courtyard complete with a garden that features over 30 species of tropical plants, a pool, hot tub, sauna, and a separate pool house where gourmet breakfasts are served on the weekends. This Corpus secret has been used by Eva Longoria and features decor that makes you feel like you stepped into a Hemingway novel.

VILLA LA CASITA

361-882-1444
www.villalacasita.com
1813 2nd St., Corpus Christi, TX 78404
Price: Moderate
Credit Cards: AE, D, MC, V

This charming early-20th-century B&B has a courtyard that keeps you looking for Douglas Fairbanks Jr. to swing down in full Zorro garb. I have never seen a place so tastefully decorated. From the subdued hues of the master bedroom to the strategically placed door in the buffet area, this B&B is fantastically outfitted—and it's moderately priced. The prosaic name, which translates into "estate of the little house," only helps by evoking images of life in La Mancha. As far as comfort goes, this B&B is relatively large (eight rooms), with two baths so you won't be tripping over anyone else.

Vacation Rentals

For those planning on spending more than five days in Corpus, renting from these condos and apartments is possibly the best way to go. Most have weekly rates, and all have a very helpful staff.

EL CONSTANTE CONDOMINIUMS

361-949-7088
www.elconstante.com
14802 Windward Dr., Corpus Christi, TX 78418
Price: Moderate to Expensive
Credit Cards: AE, D, MC, V

This out-of-the-way condo complex sports one of the nicest pools in Corpus, and you can have a two-bedroom, two-story unit with three balconies at your disposal. The location makes it easy to spend your whole vacation at the beach, and there's a BBQ pit for those who feel like showing off their mastery of the grilling arts.

GULFSTREAM CONDOMINIUMS

361-949-8061
14810 Windward Dr., Corpus Christi, TX 78418
Price: Moderate to High
Credit Cards: AE, D, MC. V

This six-story hotel offers guests club privileges at the Padre Isles Country Club as well as shuffleboard and a game room. All the suites have two bedrooms and are very nice.

ISLAND HOUSE CONDOMINIUMS

361-949-8166
15340 Leeward Dr., Corpus Christi, TX 78418
Price: Moderate
Credit Cards: AE, DC, MC, V

This place is unique for Corpus because it allows guests to rent three-bedroom suites for about the same price as the two one-bedroom and 63 two-bedroom units. This

is a fisherman's paradise, and the location makes it easy to get out and experience all that Corpus has to offer.

SURFSIDE CONDOMINIUM APARTMENTS

361-888-5391
15005 Windward Dr., Corpus Christi, TX 78418
Price: Moderate
Credit Cards: AE, D, MC, V

This condo complex has 29 two-bedroom suites and a great reputation. It has a lovely pool, allows pets, and is located mere minutes from all that Corpus has to offer. Another thing that separates Surfside from the pack is that it doesn't change its prices throughout the year. That makes life so much easier.

Camping

Although Corpus does not have a KOA campground, never fear. The best place to camp in Corpus is the Padre Island National Seashore. See the listing in the National and State Parks section (immediately preceding chapter 1) for information.

RESTAURANTS

I would be lying if I tried to paint a picture of a happy Corpus culinary community. There is a controversy raging, and it has been going on for years. It is based on the fact that Corpus has such a rich culinary tradition that can draw from its large ethnic diversity—Irish, Hispanic, Filipino, Japanese, Vietnamese, Czech, to name a few. This rich tradition has caused some of the Corpus foodies to get up in arms about the rise of the popular seafood-steakhouse-style restaurants, which they feel are homogenizing menus and turning all Corpus restaurants into the same thing. Others think this is an overreaction to a

Most likely the prettiest back alley in Texas.

minor problem. They point to the existence of good sushi bars and fantastic Mexican and Chinese restaurants as proof that diversity still exists and that menus aren't being cloned. These dining defenders also point out that seafood-steakhouse menus all aren't the same and that many incorporate South American and other elements into their recipes. Both sides do have valid points: There sure are a lot of seafood-steakhouse restaurants; but then again there are a lot of other types, too. The best bet is to try some of it all before jumping into the debate.

ANCIENT MARINER SEAFOOD RESTAURANT

361-992-7371
4366 S. Alameda St., Corpus Christi, TX 78412

Type of Food: Seafood and steak
Price: Inexpensive to Moderate
Credit Cards: AE, CB, D, DC, MC, V

With a diehard following and gumbo to write home about, the Mariner is possibly one of the best-kept secrets in Corpus. Locals rant and rave about how authentically Corpus it is; they stick up for it when someone gives a bad review. This restaurant is held close to sacred by its devotees, some of whom eat here two or three times a week.

BAMBOO GARDEN CHINESE RESTAURANT

361-993-7993
1220 Airline Rd., Corpus Christi, TX 78412
Type of Food: Chinese/Vietnamese
Price: Inexpensive to Moderate
Credit Cards: AE, D, MC, V

This is a typical Americanized Chinese food restaurant, right down to the pepper ratings denoting the spice level in dishes. It has a Vietnamese menu, too.

BLACKBEARD'S ON THE BEACH
361-884-1030
3117 Surfside Blvd., Corpus Christi, TX 78402
Type of Food: Seafood and Tex-Mex
Price: Inexpensive to Moderate
Credit Cards: AE, DC, D, MC, V

Blackbeard's is a veritable Corpus Christi landmark, especially to those who believe in the paranormal. Over the years, employees and patrons of Blackbeard's have heard strange noises emanate from the kitchen, usually the crashing of pots and pans, and seen what appeared to be an apparition of a woman wandering through the building. Some think that the ghost is a former employee who lost a piece of jewelry in a fire and died trying to retrieve it. Since 1991 Corpus Christi music legend Bobby Carter has been appearing five nights a week alongside the paranormal and in front of a mixed bag of tourists and locals who shell out for huge onion rings and good salsa.

BLACK DIAMOND OYSTER BAR
361-992-2432
7202 South Padre Island Dr., Corpus Christi, TX 78412
Type of Food: Seafood and steak
Price: Inexpensive to Moderate
Credit Cards: AE, CB, D, DC, MC, V

A favorite with the locals, this blue-collar oyster bar has one of the cheapest happy hours, best-stocked bars, and lowest wait-staff turnover. The food is made fresh and always to your order.

CITY DINER AND OYSTER BAR
361-883-1643
622 N. Water St., Corpus Christi, TX 78401
Type of Food: Diner and seafood
Price: Inexpensive to Moderate
Credit Cards: AE, DC, D, MC, V

This art-deco themed restaurant was a local favorite when it was owned and managed by Elmo Jackson. His passing has left the place searching for a public face and an identity. On the positive side is the fact that it still is well-known for its greasy-spoon aesthetic, hamburgers, shakes, and malts. However, the true gem is the Nueces snapper, a glorious helping of Gulf snapper topped with pecans and shrimp served smothered in sauce. Combine it with stuffed mushrooms and an oyster bar happy hour and it isn't unheard of to spend three or four hours at this friendly diner.

JEZEBELLES RESTAURANT
361-887-7403
Art Center of Corpus Christi
100 N. Shoreline Blvd., Corpus Christi, TX 78401
Type of Food: Lunch and brunch
Price: Moderate
Credit Cards: AE, D, MC, V

Only open from 11 AM to 3 PM, this picturesque bistro is located on the bay with a clear view of the marina. That plus the paintings from local artists on the wall makes for interesting things to look at while you wait for your food. Add a Sunday jazz brunch and you get one of the most pleasant dining destinations in Corpus.

KATZ 21 STEAK & SPIRITS
361-884-1815
www.katz21.com
317 Mesquite St. (at the corner of Lawrence), Corpus Christi, TX 78401
Type of Food: Steak and seafood
Price: Expensive to Very Expensive
Credit Cards: AE, D, MC, V

Designed as a tribute to the supper clubs of the swing era, this upscale steakhouse/

seafood restaurant has one of the best menus in the city. It features such delicious delicacies as veal scalloppini marsala and beef tenderloin medallions gorgonzola. As well as offering singly priced menu items, they also offer tier-priced meals, which are an excellent way to save money on a night out.

MAO TAI'S CHINESE RESTAURANT
361-852-8877
4601 South Padre Island Dr., Corpus Christi, TX 78411
Type of Food: Chinese
Price: Inexpensive to Moderate
Credit Cards: AE, CB, D, DC, MC, V

This low- to mid-priced Chinese restaurant is fairly typical fare (beef and broccoli, fried rice, etc.), and if you're in the mood for Chinese, it's not bad.

ORIGAMI JAPANESE CUISINE
361-993-3966
1220 Airline Rd. #150, Corpus Christi, TX 78412
Type of Food: Japanese
Price: Inexpensive to Moderate

This is one of the best sushi shops in Corpus, with a talented chef who is able to execute some of the most complicated cuts imaginable. He's so good and so precise it makes you wonder if he knows how to do blowfish.

PIER 99
361-887-0764
2822 N. Shoreline Blvd., Corpus Christi, TX 78402
Type of Food: Seafood
Price: Inexpensive to Moderate
Credit Cards: AE, DC, D, MC, V

A Greek diner offers an inviting-looking rest stop.

Near the Texas State Aquarium and USS *Lexington*, this gem of a seafood restaurant is a hit with locals and tourists alike. The reasons for their consistent popularity are the gigantic portions, homemade tartar sauce, and a deck that faces out onto the bay and provides a postcard view of the *Lexington*. It doesn't hurt that their bartender knows how to whip up a good Long Island Ice Tea or that they periodically have live music. But the real star is the food. Their menu is filled with Gulf seafood classics, and the kitchen does them all perfectly and sells them for cheap.

Q PUB

361-991-9840
www.theqpub.com
4223 S. Alameda St., Corpus Christi, TX 78412
Type of Food: Pub grub
Price: Inexpensive to Moderate
Credit Cards: AE, D, MC, V

This restaurant/bar has embraced the digital revolution so much that the house DJ doesn't spin—he points and clicks his way through the night. The food is fairly standard pub grub, and the whole environment lends itself to having a good time, especially when the house band plays on Thursday and Saturday.

REPUBLIC OF TEXAS BAR & GRILL

361-886-3515
900 N. Shoreline Blvd. (in Omni Hotel Bayfront Tower), Corpus Christi, TX 78401
Type of Food: Steak and seafood
Price: Expensive to Very Expensive
Credit Cards: AE, CB, D, DC, MC, V

Throughout this book I have tried to shy away from discussing hotel bars and restaurants for two reasons. The first is that the restaurant is rarely indicative of the local cuisine, and second, aside from the wait staff, the people you meet at the hotel bar are even less indicative of the

local culture. Even acknowledging those reservations, the Republic of Texas still deserves to be included for two reasons—it simply is one of the best restaurants in Corpus, and it is 20 stories up, providing a brilliant view of the bay and the city. As for the service—the staff knows what to do and how long not to keep you waiting. This is the place to eat in Corpus.

TAJMAHAL INDIAN RESTAURANT

361-904-0800
601 N. Shoreline Blvd. (in Bayfront Inn), Corpus Christi, TX 78401
Type of Food: Indian
Price: Inexpensive to Moderate
Credit Cards: AE, MC, V

Having just spent a whole paragraph with the exception to the rule about hotel restaurants, I feel an obligation to present the other side. The Tajmahal is thoroughly Americanized Indian food, complete with a buffet. Buffets are the enemy of authenticity; they prove that you are about as far from the reality of the cuisine as you can get. Nevertheless, there are some things refreshing about the Tajmahal. One is that it is an Indian restaurant in Corpus, one of a very few. Another is that it has lovely understated decor. The simple elegance is very nice.

WATER STREET MARKET

361-881-9448
www.waterstreetco.com
309 N. Water St., Corpus Christi, TX 78401
Type of Food: Cajun seafood, steakhouse
Price: Inexpensive to Moderate
Credit Cards: AE, D, DC, MC, V

Home to both the Water Street Seafood Company and Water Street Oyster Bar, this slightly pricey seafood restaurant first opened its doors in 1983 and within five years expanded to San Antonio. The success of Water Street—it is one of the most popular restaurants in Corpus—is based on simple statements that are paradoxically revolutionary: fresh fish that is never frozen, and sauces, dressings, and specialties made from scratch. The menu is primarily composed of standbys like seafood pasta jambalaya, mesquite chicken, and the always reliable "surf 'n' turf." The only deviations from this formula are the Embrochette Platter—oysters and shrimp wrapped together with bacon, deep fried without batter, and served over a bed of french fries with cole slaw and tartar sauce; and the Caldo Xochitl—a Mexican soup composed of chicken, garden vegetables, and rice topped with avocado and *pico de gallo*.

YARDARM RESTAURANT

361-855-8157
4310 Ocean Dr., Corpus Christi, TX 78412
Type of Food: Seafood
Price: Inexpensive to Moderate
Credit Cards: AE, CB, D, DC, MC, V

This cozy, intimate restaurant is nestled snugly into an antique house and offers a beautiful view of Corpus Christi Bay from its deck. It also has one of those unfortunate nautically inspired names (as in hang him from the) that tend to mark seafood restaurants. However, the oysters Rockefeller and snapper papillote more than make you forget about the name.

NIGHTLIFE

BOURBON STREET BAR & GRILL

361-882-2082
315 N. Chaparral St., Corpus Christi, TX 78401

This used to be a hot 18–25 dance club called Sharkey's that attracted many students from Texas A&M Corpus Christi and Del Mar. That shut down and reopened in 2006 as Bourbon Street. It now has a radically different concept; instead of wet T-shirt contests and body shots it has Texas hold 'em and FOCUS meetings (Focus on a Creative Urban Society, a Corpus Christi quality-of-life of council) and live music.

BREWSTER STREET ICE HOUSE

361-884-2739
www.brewsterstreet.net
1724 N. Tancahua St., Corpus Christi, TX 78401

This music venue / sports bar / restaurant boasts one of the largest tequila selections in the city and possibly the most beers on tap. They also bring in great bands to help support the scene.

BUCKHORN SALOON

361-776-2816
2816 Main St., Ingleside, TX 78362

This rustic bar is all the way across the bay in Ingleside. It is reputedly haunted and has a bizarre stuffed duck, with a built-in duck call that is blown by patrons. It may seem weird and strange at first, but after five or six beers it becomes a fun thing to do.

CASSIDY'S IRISH PUB

361-879-0534
601 N. Water St., Corpus Christi, TX 78401

This is an Irish pub that knows traditional Irish music isn't "Danny Boy," and that it goes back hundreds of years and involves instruments with names that are very difficult to pronounce. They also know the secrets behind pouring Guinness. This is a well-informed bar, and if you order Irish whiskey be sure to ask which one is northern Irish and which is southern. It's an interesting history lesson.

CLICK'S BILLIARDS

361-851-2680
4535 South Padre Island Dr., Corpus Christi, TX 78411

This chain of pool halls has 18 locations in 5 states, 11 of them in Texas. The Corpus location has 10 pool tables, poker three nights a week, video games, and a TV everywhere you look, usually showing some sort of sporting event. They have also taken the first steps into the world of glam photography by publishing a "Girls of Clicks" calendar.

CRAZY TIMES COMEDY CLUB
361-906-0545
5858 South Padre Island Dr., Suite 22, lower level Sunrise Mall, Corpus Christi, TX 78412

Playing host to a majority of lesser-known "road comics" and an open-mike night on Wednesday, this place helps hold the fort for South Texas comedy. If you think you have what it takes to be the next Jerry Seinfeld or Ellen DeGeneres or just want to be able to say I saw them first, then this is the place for you.

DEAD-EYE DICK'S SALOON
361-882-2192
305 N. Chaparral St., Corpus Christi, TX 78401

At Dead-Eye Dick's, the oldest and largest country nightclub in Corpus, you can expect to hear country music that embraces both the Bakersfield and the Nashville sounds. It's a good place to drink a beer if you feel that you want to have an experience that involves two-stepping and cowboy hats.

DR. ROCKIT'S BLUES BAR
361-884-7634
709 N. Chaparral St., Corpus Christi, TX 78401

This is one of the best blues bars I've ever been to. It's spacious, books great bands, the crowd gets into the music and starts dancing, and best of all, the drinks are reasonably priced. If you want to hear some great bluesy rock 'n' roll, this is the place to go. It's been around for about 15 years and shares a name with a Texas bluesman who has been around for about 50. Since the place was pretty busy, I wasn't able to find out if the bar is owned by the legendary Dr. Rockit, but even if it isn't, this place is still a good time.

HIDDEN DOOR
361-882-5002
802 S. Staples St., Corpus Christi, TX 78404

This dance club caters primarily to the gay Latino market. And it does it very well; it is recognized statewide as the best gay Latino dance club in South Texas.

HOUSE OF ROCK
361-882-7625
ww.texashouseofrock.com
511 Star St., Corpus Christi, TX 78401

This is the possibly the best live music venue in Corpus Christi. It plays host to major-name touring bands and local acts. If you want to see some fantastic musicianship, check out this bar on a Friday or Saturday night.

MARTINI BAR
361-814-2010
6601 Everhart Rd., Suite D-5, Corpus Christi, TX 78413

This swank strip-center bar books bands on the weekends, and the bar staff knows why you shake a vodka martini and stir a gin martini—it has to do with different types of distillation processes and complexity of flavors. Be careful if you order them extra dirty.

MULLIGAN'S

361-884-8190
621 N. Chaparral St., Corpus Christi, TX 78401

This is a college bar that is primarily focused on A&M students. It is an all-right place to go if you don't mind hearing about how tough a professor is or how the Islanders are doing.

MURDOCK'S

361-991-9606
2033 Airline Rd., Corpus Christi, TX 78412

This laid-back sports bar never has a cover, has good drinks that sell for cheap, and has a friendly staff. It is definitely a place to go to unwind after a long trip or meeting.

PARADISE POOL & BILLIARDS

361-852-9252
5141 Oakhurst Dr., Corpus Christi, TX 78411

This neighborhood sports bar is definitely a place to hang out with some friends, shoot some eight ball, and watch the game. The beer is always cold, the crowd friendly, and the staff smile when you walk in the door.

SIXX

361-888-7499
www.thesixx.com
1212 Leopard St., Corpus Christi, TX 78404

This gay dance club is the biggest and most famous in South Texas. That's because it offers so much—drag queens, amateur strippers, a good DJ, and cheap drinks.

Nashville vs. Bakersfield

The term "Nashville sound" describes how country music evolved from the more traditional rural-blues arrangements to a contemporary pop sound with layered orchestrations, smooth vocals, no solos, and choral backings. The man who is given the most credit for this transition is Chet Atkins, a guitar player and producer who in the mid-1950s realized that in order for country and western artists to keep up with big bands and the emerging rock scene, they would have to lose the southern working-class aspects that defined C&W. This change came to be known as "The Chet Atkins Compromise," and it helped turn country music into a multimillion-dollar industry in the sixties. It also led many artists outside Nashville to feel that country music had been reduced to a vanilla formula. This alienation and disenfranchisement of many musicians sparked a West Coast reaction known as the Bakersfield sound. As can be inferred from the name, this particular movement in country music had its origin in and around Bakersfield, California. It may seem strange to some that California would play, and continues to play, such an important part in the development of country music. However, once you realize that the Dust Bowl immigrants were headed to California and many of them settled in Bakersfield, the idea that a small Southern California town could play such a pivotal part in the evolution of country music doesn't seem so hard to understand. The main things that separated the Bakersfield sound from its eastern rival were the arrangements. While Chet Atkins was arranging Patsy Cline for strings, Buck Owens was including a lap steel guitar and twin fender telecasters in his records. Another of the main differences between Nashville country and Bakersfield came in the use of the studio. In Nashville it was not uncommon for musicians to come in to the studio and do their parts separately and let the producer mix and layer as he or she saw fit. However, in Bakersfield that idea was considered immoral. The prevailing viewpoint was the songs are recorded the same way they are played live. These two approaches to production and arrangement are still present in country music today. For further reading on the subject of Nashville vs. Bakersfield, as well as other movements in country, please see *Creating Country Music: Fabricating Authenticity*, by Richard A. Peterson.

UNDERGROUND VENUE
361-882-4004
www.myspace.com/theundergroundvenue
3101 Agnes St., Corpus, Christi TX 78405

This is a club for those into underground metal. The crowd is young, the music loud and fast, the clothes jeans and T-shirt (preferably black), and the dancing borders on fighting. Ah, to be 18 again, when it was all new and fun.

ATTRACTIONS

Performing Arts
Corpus Christi has a vibrant performing arts scene, with two internationally recognized ballets, a symphony, and one of the better-known community theater troupes in the state. All of them are worth seeing, and unlike major metropolitan orchestras or ballets, they won't set you back a bundle.

CORPUS CHRISTI BALLET
361-882-4588
www.corpuschristiballet.com
1621 N. Mesquite St., Corpus Christi, TX 78401

With a very short season, just three shows, this ballet spends much of its time working on outreach programs with local schoolchildren. They have gotten so good at it that their premiere program, balletWorks for KIDS, is nationally recognized. They also do an excellent interpretation of the holiday standby, *The Nutcracker*.

CORPUS CHRISTI CONCERT BALLET
361-854-7969
www.coastalbendballet.org
3446 S. Alameda St., Corpus Christi, TX 78411

Founded in 1976, this regional powerhouse excels at its mission of "building

Street musician with aftermarket addition to her fiddle.

tomorrow's audiences today" through a partnership with Del Mar College, a repertoire of classic and contemporary work, educational outreach programs, and free spring performances. All this work has not been without recognition: In 2000 the company was invited to perform at the Tanzsommer Dance Festival in Austria.

CORPUS CHRISTI SYMPHONY ORCHESTRA
361-883-6683 or 1-877-286-6683
www.ccsymphony.org
555 N. Carancahua St., Corpus Christi, TX 78478

It's hard to imagine what it was like for this orchestra when it first began in 1945. Back then the musicians were playing Liszt in a leaky high school gym for $25. Sixty years later they have performed for over 750,000 people, with a who's who of guest musicians including Itzhak Perlman and Joyce Yang.

HARBOR PLAYHOUSE
361-888-7469
www.harborplayhouse.com
1581 N. Chaparral St., Corpus Christi, TX 78401

Started in 1925 with a simple ad looking for performers, Harbor Playhouse has grown up. With seasons that last all the way into September and a focus primarily on musicals and comedies, this quaint little theater helps to keep the flame of culture burning in South Texas. Its location, next to the Water Garden and under the Harbor Bridge, makes it one of the most photogenic places to take in a play in Texas.

PERFORMING ARTS CENTER AT TEXAS A&M UNIVERSITY
361-825-2787
6300 Ocean Dr., Corpus Christi, TX 78412

This $18 million performance space is the pride and joy of Corpus Christi. The 1,500-seat hall was designed with one goal in mind—to be the best place on the Texas coast to hear music. The backers spared no expense making that dream a reality; they approached and consulted with world-renowned acoustic experts and Tony Award—winning theater designers in order to get things so that every note sounds good. These efforts paid off, and now this venue has a show virtually every day. Whether it's the state high school orchestra competition or a U.S. Army field band, someone will be doing a show here.

Museums
Corpus Christi has a very respectable share of museums, primarily because of the city's dedication to preserving and promoting all things local. This attitude may seem

provincial to some, but in a state with many cities that are known for paying lip service to the arts, it is admirable to see local artists displayed alongside internationally recognized luminaries at the largest art museum in town.

ART CENTER OF CORPUS CHRISTI
361-884-6406
100 N. Shoreline Blvd., Corpus Christi, TX 78401

This cultural treasure helps to promote local art by providing connoisseurs and artists with an almost completely vertically integrated art experience. From creation, to exhibition, to sale, to dining, the Art Center has a space for it all. They also have meeting and workshop space, artist studios, galleries, and a full clay studio. All of which they use to teach classes in order to help promote local art and artists. If only every city had such an organization. Another reason to visit this establishment is that the admission is free.

ART MUSEUM OF SOUTH TEXAS / CORPUS CHRISTI ART FOUNDATION
1902 N. Shoreline Blvd., Corpus Christi, TX 78401

This lovely art museum is a hidden gem in Corpus and deserves much more financial support than it receives. It has a very respectable collection of recent paintings by contemporary artists. While it doesn't have the resources to attract large touring shows or groundbreaking works, the pieces on display are definitely worth seeing.

CORPUS CHRISTI MUSEUM OF SCIENCE AND HISTORY
361-826-4667
www.ccmuseum.com
1900 N. Chaparral St., Corpus Christi, TX 78401

This museum has possibly the most ambitious mission statement of any museum in Texas: "to present the story of the cultural crossroads of the New World." It would seem that living up to this monumentally tall order would be impossible and any museum that might attempt it would inevitably be set up for failure. Fortunately that's not the case here. The exhibits not only tell the story of the colonization of the New World, but also make it enjoyable for families. The prize exhibits are the painstaking reproductions of Columbus's ships. Valued at $6.5 million apiece, these vessels were handcrafted in Spain using the same methods that produced the originals. Examples of the incredible attention to detail exhibited in their construction can be found in the facts that the lumber used to make these ships was felled in the same forests as the lumber used for the originals, the nails were hand-forged as they would have been in the 15th century, and the sails were made out of the closest materials available to what sailmakers used back then. This attention to detail doesn't stop with just the ships; the museum also has an ongoing exhibit of 15th-century cartography and navigation equipment, and on the first two Saturdays in October visitors are greeted by costumed tour guides who portray actual crew members who served under Columbus. In addition to conducting tour groups around the ships, these docents conduct catapult, crossbow, and cooking demonstrations. This is definitely the place to take children and sailors. Aspiring nautical archaeologists might also be interested, since the museum is headquarters for the internationally recognized underwater archaeology and recovery firm Ships of Discovery, which has searched for and dived in wrecks throughout the Caribbean.

TEXAS MARITIME MUSEUM
1-866-729-2469
www.texasmaritimemuseum.org
1202 Navigation Circle, Rockport, TX 78382

The mission of the Texas Maritime Museum is to educate and excite the public about the history and culture of the Texas coast, and it does a fantastic job of it. From prehistory to present day, the museum provides an admirable overview of the whole area, focusing primarily on the Coastal Bend region of Corpus Christi.

TEXAS STATE MUSEUM OF ASIAN CULTURES & EDUCATION CENTER
361-882-2641
www.asianculturesmuseum.org
1809 N. Chaparral St., Corpus Christi, TX 78401

Founded in the 1960s by an Asian antiquities collector and former teacher, this museum has the potential to be one of the best in the state. Past exhibits have included the paintings of world-famous local artist Hsiao-Hsia Tsai, the Contemporary Japanese Crafts exhibit, and the National Taiwanese Treasure Box exhibit.

TEXAS SURF MUSEUM
361-888-SURF (7873)
www.texassurfmuseum.com
309 N. Water St., Corpus Christi, TX 78401

Surfing, surfboards, and surfers is what this museum is all about. Having started out as a display on a wall at Pat Magee's Surf Shop, the Surf Museum has grown exponentially from those early days. Its collection of 35 vintage surfboards and 100-plus historic photos of Texas surfers is now housed in a 3,000-square-foot building next to the Executive Surf Club. As the museum has expanded it has grown to include a mock shop used to explain the process of shaping a surfboard and a theater that continuously plays surf movies.

THE SELENA MUSEUM

361-289-9013

5410 Leopard St., Corpus Christi, TX 78408

This museum, founded in 1998 by the late singer Selena Quintanilla-Pérez's family at the behest of their daughter's fans, is the Corpus Christi Graceland. The museum displays memorabilia from the singer's career, including her red Porsche, midriff-baring stage outfits, and gold records. In the gift shop you can get your Selena T-shirts, hats, posters, and directions to the Selena memorial on Shoreline, the Selena gravesite on Ocean, and the Selena boutique on Everhart.

USS LEXINGTON

361-888-4873

2914 N. Shoreline Blvd., Corpus Christi, TX 78402

The USS *Lexington*, or as it is affectionately known, the Blue Ghost, is the pride and joy of Corpus Christi. It was one of the last serving World War II aircraft carriers until it was decommissioned in 1990. At that time the Corpus Christi Area Economic Development Commission formed what can only be described as a task force, called Landing Force 16, to lobby the U.S. Navy to give the aged warhorse to the city. After two years and a $3 million campaign, they succeeded, and the Navy brought the Lexington to Naval Station Ingleside, its base near Corpus, and signed the *Lexington* over to the city. The *Lex* (another of its nicknames) was retrofitted with a three-story-high mega-theater, a 16-seat flight simulator, and a café. All these additions, along with popular youth group overnight camps, have helped make the *Lexington* one of the few self-supporting museums in South Texas.

Historical Homes and Landmarks

One of the things that separate the historical buildings in Corpus from those elsewhere is the lack of ostentation. Unlike San Simeon, the Bishop's Palace, or other American castles, Corpus Christi's Victorian homes are extremely subdued. While this muted aesthetic helps to define Corpus Christi, it jeopardizes the buildings. Since the historic homes of the Coastal Bend placed function over form, they do not stand out as monuments to a bygone era.

This led to the creation of the Corpus Christi Landmark Commission and a unique-for-Texas attempt at preservation. In the late 1970s the Landmark Commission started what can only be described as a historic building reservation, onto which houses were moved, called Heritage Park. The park started with just two houses—the Lichtenstein House and the Sidbury House—but soon after added a third, the Gugenheim House. The moving of houses continued throughout the '80s. Three were moved in 1982 alone; then another in '86, and the last one was moved in 1987. However, relocation would end altogether in the '90s. In fact, there hasn't been a house moved into Heritage Park in 20 years. This is despite overwhelming increases in suburban sprawl and a recently renewed interest in urban high-density living, the two main factors that threaten old buildings. For a complete listing of all Corpus Christi landmarks, historic buildings, and historical points of interest, go to www.cclandmarks.org

CHARLES BLUCHER / GEORGE BLUCHER / RICHARD BLUCHER HOUSES

123, 211, and 205 N. Carrizo St., Corpus Christi, TX 78401

These three houses were owned by three of the five Blucher brothers on an 8-acre tract they owned that was known as Blucherville. The Charles Blucher House was originally constructed for the patriarch Felix and his wife, Maria, in the 1880s. It was a single story then, the second story being added 30 years later. In keeping with the classical-revival style that dominated construction of that time, a full second-story porch was added along with the additional story. The house is now the headquarters of the Junior League. The George Blucher House is much more modest than that of his parents; it is a simple two-and-a-half-story Queen Anne cottage, with two chamfered bays on the second-story porch. It is now a privately owned bed & breakfast. The Richard Blucher House is yet another piece of revivalist architecture, with a full porch and Doric columns. Richard kept his porch to one story.

CENTENNIAL HOUSE
361-882-8691
411 N. Upper Broadway, Corpus Christi, TX 78401

This two-story coral pink house was built in 1849 by Forbes Britton and is the oldest standing structure in Corpus Christi. Like any building that has been around for close to 160 years, it has a storied history. From being used as a Confederate hospital in the Civil War to a Federal hospital and officers' mess during Reconstruction, on down to a refuge from Indian and bandit raids in the 1870s, the Centennial House has been the backdrop to the history of Texas as lived by generations of Coastal Bend residents—which is why it is one of the 11 places in Corpus Christi that are on the National Register of Historic Places.

JALUFKA-GOVATOS HOUSE
361-880-3560
Heritage Park
1513 N. Chaparral St., Corpus Christi, TX 78401

Built in the southern bungalow style in 1908 in the Irishtown section of Corpus by a Spanish-American War and World War I veteran, this house features fairly unusual paired columns on the front porch and a rusticated block foundation. It was acquired in 1987 and then moved to the Heritage Park location. Afterward it was restored by the Czech Heritage Society of South Texas, who use it for offices and meeting rooms. The nonprofit Czech Heritage Society is dedicated to preserving and maintaining the language and customs of the Czech community in South Texas.

LICHTENSTEIN HOUSE
361-880-3560
Heritage Park
1617 N. Chaparral St., Corpus Christi, TX 78401

Built in 1905 by the scion of the Lichtenstein Department Store family, this house is a model of the simplicity that can be found in the plainest Queen Anne style. Even the main defining feature, the turret with clerestory windows, shows marked restraint for late-Victorian architecture. This restraint becomes evident when the house is compared with others from the same period in Galveston or New Orleans.

To learn more about preserving endangered or threatened buildings, go to the National Register of Historic Places Web site, www.nationalregisterofhistoricplaces.com, and click on the Register Forms link. You will be taken to a list of all the State Historic Preservation offices.

LITTLES-MARTIN HOUSE

361-880-3560
Heritage Park
1519 N. Chaparral St., Corpus Christi, TX
78401

Originally the home of one of the city's first native black residents, this house now serves as the headquarters of the Corpus chapter of the NAACP. The relationship of Hattie Moore and Willis Littles to their employer John G. and Marie Stella Kenedy, local ranchers, can only be described as surprisingly benevolent. When the Littleses were baptized as the first black Catholics in Corpus Christi, and two of the few in all Texas, the Kenedys were their godparents. And after the Littleses retired, the Kenedys gave them the house. The

A Texas rarity: a three-story historic home.

house remained in the Littles family until 1983, when the city acquired it and moved it to Heritage Park. This Queen Anne–style cottage has some striking architectural details, such as the tigerwood mantel in the living room. Tigerwood, or Nigerian walnut, is native to West Africa. Then there is the beveled siding, a rare feature on any home of the period, and even rarer on homes owned by blacks. The pier-and-beam foundation, in contrast, is a very common method of constructing houses in areas prone to flooding.

MERRIMAN-BOBYS HOUSE

361-880-3560
Heritage Park
1521 N. Chaparral St., Corpus Christi, TX 78401

This, the second-oldest house in Corpus, was used as a hospital during the Civil War and then again during the yellow fever epidemic of 1867. It also is one of the more unusual structures in Corpus, with its three gables giving it the appearance of three houses pushed together. This unique roof came about as additions were built over the years.

OLD BAYVIEW CEMETERY

Waco and W. Broadway, Corpus Christi, TX 78401

This cemetery, the first in Corpus Christi, was established in 1845 after the steamship *Dayton* exploded, killing 10 men, and General Zachary Taylor found he lacked a proper burial ground. One of the more interesting aspects of the cemetery is its classification of the deceased into black, white, Hispanic, and Irish.

SIDBURY HOUSE

361-883-9352
Heritage Park 1609 N. Chaparral St.,
Corpus Christi, TX 78401

Built in 1893 by rancher, banker, lumber company manager, civic leader, and frontierswoman Charlotte Sidbury, this house is one of the few surviving examples of high-Victorian architecture in Corpus. It was designed with all the elements of Queen Anne style—asymmetry, irregular outlines, verandas, balconies, and gables. What sets it apart from its contemporaries farther up the coast are the unusual details such as the Moorish arch over the front steps. Detailed woodworking on the porch contributes to the Victorian gingerbread appearance.

WARD-MCCAMPBELL HOUSE

1501 N. Chaparral St., Corpus Christi, TX 78401

When construction was completed in 1908, this house sat a few feet from Corpus Christi Bay, smack in the middle of old Irishtown. In 1919 a hurricane came and cut the city in two, isolating the lowlands of Irishtown from the high grounds of the bluff. It is said that Mary Ward McCampbell and her three sons retreated to the second-story porch as dead animals and entire houses floated by in the storm surge. The next year Mary McCampbell died of pneumonia that she supposedly contracted during the hurricane. The house was donated to the city in 1983 and is now used as the offices and meeting rooms for Irish Cultural House Inc., a nonprofit dedicated to informing and educating the public about the Irish influence on Corpus and the Coastal Bend.

Zoos and Aquariums

The city has one of the best aquariums in the state and one of the most outstanding botanical gardens on the Texas coast. Both are well worth a visit.

SOUTH TEXAS BOTANICAL GARDENS & NATURE CENTER

361-852-2100
www.stxbot.org
8545 S. Staples St., Corpus Christi, TX
78413

With thousands of species of plants and animals, this top-five tourist destination also happens to be one of the most romantic spots in all Corpus. Combine that with outreach programs like Bonsai for Beginners or the Songbird Migration Field Trip and you start to understand why this remains a favorite place for wedding photographers, school field trips, retirees, and almost everyone else in Corpus and the Coastal Bend.

TEXAS STATE AQUARIUM

361-881-1200 OR 1-800-477-GULF (4853)
www.texasstateaquarium.org
2710 N. Shoreline Blvd., Corpus Christi Beach, TX 78402

After passing through a Gulf of Mexico–themed courtyard you walk under a waterfall and meet docents who make you understand why this was voted the "Best of the Best" by the *Corpus Christi Caller Times*. With 12 daily presentations covering everything from dolphin training, getting to know the North American river otter, and touching sharks and rays, the state aquarium has something for almost everyone. The best of these programs would have to be the Dolphin Trainer for a Day, in which anyone over the age of 13 can spend a morning working with the dolphin trainers.

SPORTS AND RECREATION

While Corpus Christi lacks major league teams in all major televised sports (baseball, football, basketball, and hockey), it doesn't lack major league talent. And the absence of major league money makes the games that much more enjoyable. Personally I find it hard to go to a game where the athletes drive cars that cost as much as homes and live in mansions with bodyguards. Minor-league players are still the working-class boys trying to make good, they still talk to you at the bars, and are flattered if you ask for an autograph.

CORPUS CHRISTI HOOKS (AA AFFILIATE OF THE HOUSTON ASTROS)

361-561-4665
www.cchooks.com
734 E. Port Ave. (in the middle of downtown just off TX 181, by Bayfront Science Park), Corpus Christi, TX 78401

Nothing can be as American as minor league baseball. Kids 18 and 19 years old bouncing through the countryside in rattletrap buses, playing games for meal money and the hope that one day they'll get the call to go up to "the show." From a fan's perspective, this is where baseball is still true, where the love between a team and its city is still earnest and real, and tickets and concessions are still affordable. For what you would spend taking your family to one major league game and sitting in the upper deck, you could take 20 of your closest friends to a minor league game and get some of the best seats in the house, especially since the tickets cost $5 or $10 apiece. And in a stadium this size, even the $5 general admission seating puts you close to the action. One of the differences between minor and major league ball is the length of the season. The minor league seasons aren't as long, so the majors can call minor league players up for the push to the playoffs. This means that the Hooks play from April until the beginning of September. They also don't go into extra innings, which means their games can end in ties. Another difference is that because of the relatively sparser attendance for minor league games, the management has peculiar promotions, giving away everything from new cars to pillowcases.

CORPUS CHRISTI RAYZ

361-814-7825
www.ccrayz.com
American Bank Center
1901 N. Shoreline Blvd., Corpus Christi,
TX 78401

Ice hockey is truly one of the most beautiful of all sports. The grace and power of the athletes combined with the fast-paced ferocity make for one fantastic night out. Paradoxically, all of the reasons to see a hockey game live make it almost impossible to watch on television. However, the NHL has said they are working on ways to make it more telegenic. It's probably a good idea to see a game before TV timeouts and instant replays start dominating it, and if you are going, go to a minor league game. You can still afford to eat, drink, and buy a T-shirt or a hat without worrying about making next month's rent or mortgage payment. The Rayz season runs from mid-October until mid-April. Tickets run

The official mascot of the city of Corpus Christi.

from $10 to $27, and games are played at the American Bank Center, which is on Corpus Christi Bay in the Bayfront Science Park just off TX 181. The promotions at Rayz games are almost unbelievable: free air conditioners, diamond rings, gasoline, high-definition TV sets—even guest Tahitian dancers—among other things. My personal favorite is the power-play promotion: Every time the Rayz score a goal during a power play, the concession stand drops beer prices to $2.

Golf

With seven 18-hole courses, none of them with a par higher than 72, Corpus is fairly well set when it comes to golf. Almost all the courses are either public or offer some sort of reciprocal guest policy. However, it is best to ask about the particulars regarding those policies before showing up. Some courses even have access policies with local hotels and bed & breakfasts.

CORPUS CHRISTI COUNTRY CLUB
361-991-7870
6300 Everhart Rd., Corpus Christi, TX 78413

This private, 18-hole, par-72 course has a fairly odd dress code—collared shirts and Bermuda shorts are required. Denim is not allowed. It also has wide-open fairways with a major wind factor. It does have a reciprocal guest policy.

GABE LOZANO SENIOR GOLF COURSE
361-883-3696
4401 Old Brownsville Rd., Corpus Christi, TX 78405

This fairly demanding private, 18-hole, par 4 is a great place to work on shot accuracy. It has water hazards on most of the holes and sand bunkers on the fairways and around the greens. Since it's a public

course it has a fairly liberal dress code (shirt and shoes required).

KINGS CROSSING GOLF & COUNTRY CLUB
361-994-1395
6201 Oso Pkwy., Corpus Christi, TX 78414

Built on rolling terrain, this private, 18-hole, par-72 links-style course is populated with more doglegs than dogwoods. It also has a collared shirt, no-cutoffs policy. They are cool with denim, but the reciprocal policy is limited to clubs within 75 miles of Corpus.

OSO BEACH MUNICIPAL GOLF COURSE
361-991-5351
5601 S. Alameda St., Corpus Christi, TX 78412

This public, 18-hole, par 3 is one of the more picturesque courses in Corpus. Lined by trees, with sand bunkers throughout and water hazards on the back nine, this could be an archetype of a golf course—until you get to No. 13, that is; this one requires a difficult tee shot into a south wind over water. Blame John Bredemus for that one; he designed the course in 1938. The dress code simply requires shirt and shoes.

PADRE ISLES COUNTRY CLUB
361-949-8006
14353 Commodore Dr., Corpus Christi, TX 78418

In 1971 Bruce Littell had the idea of building a golf course on an island surrounded by 40 acres of water. One can only think it's because he really liked shooting over water hazards. Fortunately, someone convinced him that not every hole needs a water hazard—so he limited those to just 15 out of the 18 at this semiprivate par 4. They also require collared shirts and Bermuda shorts and don't allow denim. And one of the things that puts the semi in semi-private is that they have a standing agreement with Gulfstream condominiums that their guests can pay a small fee for access to the club.

PHARAOHS COUNTRY CLUB
361-991-2477
7111 Pharaoh Dr., Corpus Christi, TX 78412

This is one of the more enjoyable courses in Corpus. It's all flat, with minimal water hazards, which is why it is a par 70. It also has a liberal dress code of no tank tops or cutoffs.

RIVER HILLS COUNTRY CLUB
361-387-3563
Hwy. 624, River Hill Dr., Corpus Christi, TX 78426

When this course first opened in 1960, it was only nine holes designed by Warren Cantrell. Five years later the back nine were added. These holes don't feel like an addition, however, because of the skill of Leon Howard, who was able to expand the vision of the course without sacrificing the play. Admittedly the fairways on this par 3 may be a bit narrow, but it helps make the course a little more challenging than the rest in Corpus. The dress code is anti-denim, pro—collared shirt, and has that weird Bermuda shorts requirement. They also offer reciprocal play.

Outdoors
Corpus Christi is an outdoors-lover's dream. The metro area is unique in that it has a fairly small land square footage—154.6 square miles—and a fairly large water square mileage, of 305.6. This makes it possible to ride your bike almost anywhere in the city and water will always be close by. On top of that, the city has invested millions in turning those 154.6

square miles of land into parks. With 200-plus neighborhood parks, the Padre Island National Seashore, and the most beautiful bay in Texas, Corpus is adamant about having things to do outdoors.

COLE PARK
361-561-0253
1526 Ocean Dr., Corpus Christi, TX 78404

This 43-acre park sits right on the bay and is a must for anyone with young children. It has a massive, repeat *massive*, playground. It also offers things for adults to do, with hike-and-bike trails, a fishing pier, and a gazebo for resting in the shade.

CORPUS CHRISTI BAY TRAIL
Ocean Drive to Texas A&M Corpus Christi

This 8-mile scenic walkway stretches along Corpus Christi Bay, Oso Bay, Cayo del Oso, and Oso Creek. It runs right by the majority of tourist destinations in the city, the Art Museum of South Texas, the Museum of Science and History, the Harbor Playhouse, Cole Park, etc. It's one of the nicest ways to get where you want to go.

KING RANCH
www.king-ranch.com
www.krsaddleshop.com

This 825,000-acre ranch, in four major divisions sprawling south and west of Corpus Christi, is recognized as a national historic landmark and is considered the birthplace of the American ranching industry, American quarter horse, and the Santa Gertrudis breed of cattle. It is one of the largest ranches in the world and is so well-known that Ford trucks issued a King Ranch edition F-150 pickup, Colt Firearms issued a King Ranch commemorative pistol, and Beretta has a special King Ranch shotgun. Over the years the King Ranch has diversified from its core business of raising horses and cattle. Don't get me wrong—they still are a working ranch; in fact, this is home to sixty thousand head of cattle and some three hundred quarter horses—two of the largest herds in the state. In addition to this they have developed a brisk high-end outdoor-wear business. They also conduct guided nature/historic tours and hunts.

KING RANCH VISITOR CENTER
361-565-1344
Hwy. 141 West, Kingsville, TX 78364

KING RANCH MUSEUM
405 N. Sixth St., Kingsville, TX 78364

KING RANCH SADDLE SHOP
1-800-282-KING
201 E. Kleberg Ave., Kingsville, TX 78364

EVENTS

The Corpus Christi area is home to many different festivals. Quite a few of them have eating competitions. Whether it is raw oysters, jalapeños, or rattlesnake, if you can eat it there is probably a competition for it in this part of Texas, along with plenty of serious competitive eaters. So if you want to meet someone who just might be crowned the next Hot Dog Eating Champion of the World at Coney Island on July 4, these are the places to start looking.

January

ROCKPORT GOSPEL MUSIC FESTIVAL
First weekend in January
361-790-1105
www.rockportgospelforce.org/festival

This is the premiere gospel music festival in the state; it annually brings more than 30 acts to Rockport, about 30 miles northeast of Corpus, for a weekend of singing and praise. Many of the performers are rightly famous in the world of gospel music, often appearing on videos like the Gaither Homecoming series. In addition to gospel the festival includes fantastic bluegrass acts.

BOAR'S HEAD YULETIDE FESTIVAL
January 6-7
361-854-3044

This pageant recreates early English Christmas festivals and is definitely worth going to, if only to see what Christmas looked like hundreds of years ago.

NUECES COUNTY JR. LIVESTOCK SHOW & RODEO
Third week of January
361-387-5395

The phrase "livestock show" is fairly misleading; the only showing being done is to judges and buyers. The basic premise behind this is that kids raise an animal for about a year, take it to a competition where it is judged, and then someone buys it at auction. The whole thing is designed to help students get college scholarships. The rodeo isn't much—no bull riding or bronc busting—but then again, it is a Junior rodeo, and all the money raised goes to help FFA, FHA, and 4-H students go to college.

February

BOUNTIFUL BOWL POTTERY FAIR
First Saturday in February
Rockport Fulton High School
361-729-5352

Local potters display their wares in the RFHS commons area for sale to the public. It's possible to pick up a very beautiful piece for a fairly low price here.

WHOOPING CRANE CELEBRATION
Third weekend in February
1-800-45-COAST

A young bride gets ready for wedding pictures on the beach. Places up and down the Texas coast are used as backdrops for wedding shots all year long.

With boating trips to view the endangered migratory birds, a trade show, and world-renowned speakers, this is a must for birders.

March

FULTON HARBOR OYSTER FEST
First weekend in March
361-729-2388

This March celebration features competitions for raw oyster eating, oyster shucking, and oyster decorating, as well as live music, dancing, and arts and crafts.

KINGSVILLE–SOUTH TEXAS RANCHING HERITAGE FESTIVAL
First weekend in March
361-592-6438

This is the festival for anyone who has ever wanted to be a cowboy, likes cowboys, or wants to know what life was like on a working ranch in the late 1800s. The event has workshops on Dutch-oven cooking, chuck wagon demonstrations, live music, cowboy poets, ranch-horse competitions, ranch-hand rodeo, and a Wild West shootout—just about all the romance of the Old West.

TEXAS SAND FEST
March 20–April 1
361-749-2500

This huge event brings master and amateur sand sculptors from around the world to the beaches around Corpus Christi to see who has the skills to be number one.

CZECH HERITAGE FESTIVAL
March 24
361-882-9226

The name says it all: This is a celebration of all things Czech, especially food and music. The bands play traditional Czech music—polkas, waltzes, folk songs—as well as 1950s and '60s rock songs and country music. There are also Czech dancers and a "grand march." And you don't even have to be Czech—a board member of the Czech Heritage Society of South Texas who is one of the main organizers for the event is Scots-Irish. She simply fell in love with the culture and now wants to share it with everyone she can.

ST. PATRICK'S DAY PARADE AND DANCE
March 17

Corpus Christi is one of the few Texas towns that had a strong Irish influence, and its St. Paddy's Day parties are always a blast, especially since they fall during or just before spring break for the local colleges.

FESTIVAL OF THE ARTS
March 30–April 1
361-826-3416

This free show at Heritage Park is a fairly new celebration of the arts—it's only in its fifth year—and features performances by local musicians and nationally recognized visual artists.

PORTLAND WINDFEST
March 29–April 1
361-643-2475
www.windfest.org

This four-day celebration will leave you exhausted. It features everything from fireworks to carnival rides, as well as stunt teams, puppet shows, a beauty pageant, live music, cookoffs, and basketball, horseshoe, and washer tournaments—and much more. There is almost too much to do in just one long weekend, which is why on Saturday the festival opens at 9 AM and closes at midnight.

April

TEXAS GREAT BIRDING CLASSIC
April 15–22
1-800-766-BEACH

For the last 10 years Texas Parks and Wildlife and the Gulf Coast Bird Observatory have teamed up to run a competitive birding tournament. In that time they have raised over $500,000 for conservation purposes. These classics bring thousands of birding tourists down to check things off their life lists and compete in the All Adult, Glider (14-to-18-year-old), Roughwings (under 14), Big Sit! and Outta-Sight Song Birder tournaments. (Fun fact: the Outta-Sight tournament is for blind people.) This is a team-based competition, and the teams who win the various tournaments get to decide where a total of $51,000 in conservation money goes.

BUCCANEER DAYS
April 25–May 7
361-882-3242
www.bucdays.com

To commemorate the days of sailing ships and Jean Laffite, Corpus holds a carnival complete with fireworks, regattas, two parades, live music, a rodeo, a carnival,

BBQ cookoff, a coronation, and various other events.

CRUISE YOUR RIDE TO INGLESIDE

Last weekend in April
1-888-899-2906
www.inglesidetxchamber.com/carshow

This is a one-of-a-kind event: A combined car, bicycle, motorcycle, low-rider, and airplane show. It features a Rod Run, Cruisin' Parade, Sock Hop, and award ceremony for the audience-judged best cars.

May

NISSAN VELOCITY GAMES / U.S. OPEN WINDSURFING & KITEBOARDING CHAMPIONSHIP

Memorial Day weekend
361-888-7500
www.velocitygames.com

Started in 1989 as the U.S. Open Wind-surfing Regatta, this event is known throughout the world of extreme sports as one of the best in the country. With a location that annually has wind speeds of over 25 mph and plenty of sunshine, hip places to hang in between sessions, and $35,000 in prize money, is it any wonder that both professional and amateur wind surfers, kiteboarders, and skateboarders from all around the world flock to Corpus every Memorial Day weekend. It's always interesting to watch these athletes and see what heights, both literal and figurative, they'll push themselves to.

FREER RATTLESNAKE ROUNDUP

Second weekend in May
361-394-6891
www.freerrattlesnake.com

This is possibly one of the stranger festivals in Texas. It is a celebration of the rattlesnake and all things dealing with that feared reptile. It also happens to be one of the best festivals for country music in the state, attracting such top-tier talent as Trisha Yearwood, Diamond Rio, Mark Chestnut, John Michael Montgomery, and Asleep at the Wheel, among others.

BEACH TO BAY RELAY MARATHON

May 19
361-881-6166
www.beachtobayrelay.com

This 32-year-old, 26-mile, six-person relay race is the largest and most prestigious relay marathon in the country. It has more than 20 divisions, covering everything from elementary school to over-60. It is interesting to watch, and all the money it generates goes to charity.

THIRD COAST FISHING TOURNAMENT

Memorial Day weekend
361-992-5152
www.winthirdcoast.com

This amateur tournament offers a $5,000 prize for the heaviest redfish and $1,000 for heaviest trout and flounder and is run by the charity Young Life, "a nondenominational, Christian, non-profit organization that is committed to introducing adolescents to Jesus Christ and helping them to grow in their faith."

ROCKPORT FESTIVAL OF WINES

Memorial Day weekend
361-729-1271
www.texasmaritimemuseum.org

This event can best be summed up as two days of wine tasting, cooking demonstrations, and entertainment at the Texas Maritime Museum, one of the more interesting museums in the state.

Kiteboarders get ready to show why they're the new kings of extreme.

June

WATER STREET MARKET MUSIC & ART FEST

First weekend in June
www.executivesurfclub.com/records
361-882-2364

This annual festival draws big-name performers, as well as artists and vendors from all across the state, for three days of music and fun. The festival also serves as the induction ceremony for the South Texas Walk of Fame, a memorial to all the great musicians who live in or came from South Texas.

ARANSAS PASS SHRIMPOREE

First week of June
361-758-2750 or 1-800-633-3028
www.aransaspass.org/shrimporee

This is a celebration of the shrimp, and the Aransas Pass Chamber of Commerce does it up right—music, carnival rides, a petting zoo, cooking competition, and a parade. If you like shrimp, this is the place to be.

C-101 C-SCULPTURES

Second Saturday in June
361-289-0111 x132
www.c101.com

This is essentially a beach party sponsored by local hard-rock station C101. It features a sand castle / sculpture competition with cash prizes, beach volleyball, and live music.

July

ROCKPORT ART FESTIVAL

First weekend in July
361-729-5519

The first weekend of July finds Rockport turned into a juried art bazaar, with booth after booth of pottery, watercolors, woodwork, sculptures, and more, all of it in consideration for the grand prize.

PORT ARANSAS DEEP SEA ROUNDUP

First weekend of July
www.deepsearoundup.com

This is the oldest and biggest fishing tournament in Texas. It has divisions for pier and bay fishing. It also has a polygraph requirement: If the tournament chairman thinks you are telling a fish story, he or she has the ability to compel you to take a lie-detector test. Refusal to take the polygraph results in automatic disqualification.

August

CORPUS CHRISTI KENNEL CLUB: ALL BREED DOG SHOW

Second Saturday in August
361-884-9445

This is supposed to be about dogs, the celebration of man's best friend, and the pursuit of perfection. Now, to some this may not seem to be the most exciting thing in the world, but once you experience it and meet the people, you realize just how surreal the world of dog shows is. This is definitely worth going to.

FIESTA EN LA PLAYA

Late August
361-729-8773

This event helps to raise money for Rockport/Fulton area kids leaving for their first year of college. They do this with tamale and jalapeño and macho leg contests.

September

BAYFEST

Last weekend in September
361-887-0868

This three-day party is thrown every year on the bay front and draws musicians and performers from all over the state. It has things to do for the whole family and includes a special area just for children, appropriately named KidsFest.

Impromptu beach folk art.

ROCKPORT HUMMER/BIRD CELEBRATION

Second weekend in September
361-729-6445 or 1-800-242-0071
E-mail: hummer@rockport1.org

This is a series of workshops and birding trips timed to coincide with the bird migrations. It features workshops like "Chimney Swifts: Why We Should Care" and "Damselflies: the Other Dragon Flies." All are held at the Rockport-Fulton High School. Trip costs are separate, but the organizers make sure that participants who pay are taken by boat and by bus to places that are guaranteed to have hummingbirds. In addition to watching, the festival organizers make sure that birds get bands to track the migration.

CONQUER THE COAST

September 30
361-883-4517

Thrown in the midst of Bayfest, this multi-course bike race is famous among bicycle enthusiasts in the state, possibly because of the optional 18-mile time trial section in the middle of the 65-mile course. It also has a 25-mile "short course."

CELEBRATION OF FLIGHT HAWK WATCH

September 27–30
361-241-2617

This is one of the best places to see hawks in the United States. From August to November, more than a million broad-winged hawks, turkey vultures, Mississippi and Swainson's hawks all descend into the area around Corpus. Hawk Watch International throws a three-day celebration of the animals at the end of September, when the broad-winged hawk migration is in full effect, a time of year that turns the Corpus Christi area into the single-largest gathering place for hawks in North America.

October

ROCKPORT SEAFAIR AND GUMBO COOK-OFF

First weekend in October
361-729-6445
www.rockportseafair.com/gumbo.html

Some of the best gumbo chefs in the state come to see who has the right stuff. If you don't know a roux from a roof or boudin from bisque, this is a good place to get a primer on Creole and Cajun cooking.

TEXAS JAZZ FESTIVAL

Third weekend in October
www.texasjazz-fest.org
361-992-9428

This is the biggest jazz festival in the state, and it is not unheard of for major names—think Wynton Marsalis—to drop by and see what the Lone Star State has cooking.

INGLESIDE ROUND UP DAYS
Last weekend in October
1-888-899-2906
www.roundupdays.org

Started in 1974 but fashioned after the roundups of the 1800s, this country-themed carnival features a parade, softball tournament, cookoff, music, beauty pageant, and talent show, as well as a horseshoe tournament. For 32 years it was held each May, but apparently people decided that 90-degree springs are not the best time to have outdoor festivals, so they moved it to October.

November

GEORGEWEST STORYFEST
First weekend in November
361-449-2481 or 1-888-600-3121
www.georgeweststoryfest.org

This is a celebration of the oldest form of human entertainment—storytelling. Organizers aren't very picky about what type of story is told, as long as it entertains the crowd. This festival is also host to the Texas Liars Championship, which brings out the biggest acts in the country. When the hot air finally dissipates, you might find yourself listening to some folk songs, cowboy poetry, and Gospel stories.

KING RANCH RANCH-HAND BREAKFAST
Third Saturday in November
1-800-333-5032

This is an authentic ranch-style breakfast served in the weather off the back of a chuck wagon.

December

INGLESIDE RENAISSANCE FAIRE
First weekend in December
361-776-2906
www.renfaireingleside.org

This small weekend-long fair is filled with anachronistic people, a jubilant environment, and few tourists. This is not to be confused with the much longer and larger Texas Renaissance Faire, which is held in Plantersville and has been going strongly for 30-plus years.

LA POSADA DE KINGSVILLE
December 1
888-333-5032

This is the Kingsville version of the tree ceremony / light parade. They do things different here. They have a huge forest of trees that have already been decorated, live music, and a birding festival.

HARBOR LIGHTS FESTIVAL & BOAT PARADE
December 1
361-985-1555

A description of this festival sounds like a five-year-old's dream come true. It has a laser light show, a gingerbread and holiday tree village, and an illuminated fleet that makes a pass by. The whole thing is capped by the lighting of the tree.

ROCKPORT TREE LIGHTING & BOAT PARADE
December 6
361-729-6445

This annual tradition is a variation of the sailing of the fleet—it has a parade that includes powerboats, sailboats, and fishing boats. The children's Christmas tree is lit, and there is live music, an art sale, and an appearance by Santa Claus.

Gambling

CORPUS CHRISTI DOG TRACK

361-289-9333
5302 Leopard St., Corpus Christi, TX 78
www.corpuschristidogs.com

This track has 13 races a day, plus simul-
casts from all over the country. If you are
in the mood to gamble, this is a fairly good
place to do it. The human tellers are
knowledgeable, the automated betting very
user-friendly, and the track publishes an
easy-to-read how-to-bet guide. They also
have special matinees on Memorial,
Independence, and Labor Day weekends.
Regular race times are Wednesday at 1:30;
Thursday, 7:30 PM; Friday, 7:30 PM;
Saturday, 1:30 and 7:30; and Sunday, 1:30.

TEXAS TREASURE CASINO

(Departs from Port Aransas daily)
1-866-468-5825
www.texastreasure.com

This is the second attempt by this corporation to operate gambling cruises on the
Texas coast. Their first home port was
Freeport, 150 miles to the northeast, and
they couldn't make it work there. So in
2002 they moved the operation down to
the Corpus Christi area. For the last five
years they have been running six-hour
cruises twice daily and raking in the
dough. However, they might be facing
some competition. Another cruise ship is
set to open up shop in Freeport, although
delays have pushed the starting date to July
2007. So for now, the only place to get on a

A mysterious, buildingless concrete foundation stretches between a roadside and the beach.

slow boat to nowhere so you might win some money is here.

SHOPPING AND SERVICES

Corpus is filled with outlets of almost all the major national chains, and it seems silly to do a write-up on a store that sells the same products in Boston that it does in Texas. So I avoided national brands in favor of smaller local ones.

Stores

ARTITUDE
361-993-6882
5433 Staples St., Suite H, Corpus Christi, TX 78411

This is a bead shop where you can buy all the things you need to make your own jewelry, except for the gems. The staff is friendly and helpful and can explain techniques you may not be familiar with.

COMICS PLUS
361-992-3616
5425 South Padre Island Dr. #145, Corpus Christi, TX 78411

This family-friendly comics shop is heavily involved in the comics in the classroom movement, which helps to show that comics can be used to teach as well as entertain. Their sample lesson plans are geared toward primary education.

COTTAGE SHOP
361-694-4798
www.dchstx.org
3533 S. Alameda St., Corpus Christi, TX 78401

This is the resale shop for Driscoll Children's Hospital, a small nonprofit that makes a difference in the lives of so many. The resale shop is housed in an old classroom building behind the rehab building

and in front of the parking garage. The selection of items is fairly balanced between the new and nearly new. This is because local merchants regularly make donations.

FAMILY CHRISTIAN STORE
361-992-7717
www.familychristian.com
4938 S. Staples #B5, Corpus Christi, TX 78415

This is the location for all your religious needs. T-shirts, hats, Bibles, crosses, and more. They even sell a crown of thorns replica.

FLOUR BLUFF FEED AND GENERAL STORE
361-937-5965
3805 Waldron Rd., Corpus Christi, TX 78418

If you really want to see what Texas is all about, come here. They sell the essentials for farm life—things like hay, No. 10 yellow corn, and birdshot. This is truly worth stopping in and seeing.

FOUR CHICKS IN THE PARK
361-854-4446
www.fourchicksinthepark.com
3810 S. Alameda St., Corpus Christi, TX 78411

This is a boutique that specializes in general women's clothing and accessories with sequins and beads. Their designers are contemporary—my flat in London, Evelyn, Archipelago—and the clothes perfectly suited for everyday wear.

HALF PRICE BOOKS
361-991-4494
www.halfpricebooks.com
5425 South Padre Island Dr # 185, Corpus Christi, TX 78411

This is the Corpus affiliate of the largest, and some say best, discount bookstore in Texas. They have stores in almost every major city, with extremely competitive prices. It is not unusual for people to spend hours in here looking through the odds and ends of old books only to find a $5 copy of something they always wanted but didn't know existed.

JACK ENGLISH MENSWEAR
361-853-0361
921 N. Chaparral St., Corpus Christi, TX 78401

This is one classy store—seersucker suits and alligator belts. Damn, they can even make me look good. If you don't mind dropping some serious cash on your clothes, then this is the place to be. These guys can put you in a suit that will rival Cary Grant in *North by Northwest*, Bogart in *Casablanca*, or George Clooney in *Ocean's Eleven*.

MERCI BELLA
361-993-5999
4254 S. Alameda St., Corpus Christi, TX 78412

The owner of this boutique is an ovarian cancer survivor who does her best to raise awareness of ovarian cancer in the community. In the past she has organized fashion shows that featured her own designs. In addition to selling clothes designed by the owner, this store sells accessories with a down-to-earth and full-of-love vibe—things like belts with mosaic peace signs and bags with floral prints on them.

MOSAIC
361-991-8300
www.mosiacfashionwithsole.com
E-mail: katharineguerra@hotmail.com
5017 Saratoga Blvd., Suite 121, Corpus Christi, TX 78413

This store specializes in current and contemporary styles and brands like Ugg and J Lo. It proudly displays a picture of Paris Hilton visiting the store on its Web site. This is for those who want to be on or in front of the cutting edge.

PHAR FETCHT
361-887-8916
www.myspace.com/phar_fetcht
E-mail: pharfetcht@yahoo.com
#533 505 S. Water St. (behind the memorial coliseum at the center), Corpus Christi, TX 78401

This small store specializes in "Art Klothing & Kulture," which is an interesting way of describing small designers who use vintage patterns and big, bold graphics. This is most definitely one of the hippest shops in Corpus, primarily because it specializes in rock/psycho-billy gear. It also is the place to go if you are looking for information on the best shows in Corpus.

POLLYANNA
361-985-9161
www.pollyannacc.com
Crossroads Village #4, Corpus Christi, TX 78412

This women's-wear shop has a wide selection of beautiful gowns and gorgeous dresses, all of which look absolutely stunning. It is a favorite of the local society set, because now they don't have to make that emergency drive to Houston for a new dress.

ROSE'S ORIENTAL PRODUCTS
361-937-3995
820 Waldron Rd., Suite D, Corpus Christi, TX 78418

This store specializes in Philippine products. Whether it is food, music, movies, or furniture, you can expand your knowledge about the Philippines by visiting here as

Careful, she bites.

well as pick up some of your daily necessities. If you are looking for a place where you can get a bamboo tree, bubble gum, and a kinetic dolphin sculpture, then this is for you.

SEASIDE STAINED GLASS

361-853-4803
www.seasidestainedglass.com
6733 Weber Rd., Corpus Christi, TX 78413

This art gallery/studio specializes in stained glass and mosaic. They have classes, workshops, supplies, and everything you need to bring out your artistic side. They even offer a half-day stained-glass workshop, with all supplies provided, for one low cost.

SUN HARVEST FARMS

361-993-2850
1440 Airline Rd., Corpus Christi, TX 78412

Think of this as Corpus's home-grown Whole Foods. They specialize in vegetarian, organic, and natural foods, plus they are a fair-trade establishment. If you want to buy food that makes you feel good and good about yourself, this is the best place to go in Corpus.

WILLIAMS FASHION SHOES

361-851-0094
www.williams-shoes.com
E-mail: william@williams-shoes.com
3849 S. Alameda St., Corpus Christi, TX 78411

This high-end shoe store is geared primarily toward the more sophisticated consumer. With brand names like Lucchese, Cole Haan, and Sesto Meucci and styles that tend toward understated elegance, this is definitely the place to go if your luggage is in Anchorage and you need to buy a pair of shoes for tomorrow's big meeting.

Malls

Ah, shopping malls. Nothing can be so American. The teenagers, the fast food, the loud music and flashing lights emanating from the video arcade—these things never die. They are a part of you always and forever. Malls are a beautiful window to view the community through. So much can be learned about communities from what is sold and what is bought. Books and jewelry can be used to deduce the political and religious beliefs, the food court is a study in eating habits, and the record store charts the taste in music, just to name a few. Malls are a sociological field day. Fortunately for the amateur sociologists and people watchers, Corpus has two big ones. This will allow you to do a contrast-and-compare while you look for just the right shoes to pull off that outfit.

PADRE STAPLES MALL

361-991-5718
5488 South Padre Island Dr., Corpus Christi, TX 78411

SUNRISE MALL

361-994-4867
www.sunrise-mall.net
5858 South Padre Island Dr., Corpus Christi, TX 78412

Boats in harbor wait to go out.

3

SOUTH PADRE ISLAND

Snowbirds and Spring Break

South Padre Island (or "South Padre," as it's often called) has a fairly quiet history; it was discovered in 1519 by the Spanish explorer Alonso Álvarez de Pineda who named it Isla Blanca, or White Island. Pineda said that the land was inhabited by giants, although most historians believe he was simply referring to the Karankawa Indians who stayed on the island during the summers to fish. Over the years many a Spanish ship ran aground on what was then called Isla Blanca, some of them heavy with treasure. The most famous of these wrecks occurred in 1553 when three ships wrecked and were abandoned by some three hundred crew and passengers. After struggling to survive for six days, they were surrounded by a hundred or more heavily armed Indians who proceeded to barrage them with arrows. This forced the Spaniards to flee southward; only two survived the journey. The next documented visit by a European to what would become South Padre was in 1804 when Father José Nicolás Ballí, the man for whom Padre Island is named, founded a mission called Rancho Santa Cruz. In between converting souls, Father Ballí found time to raise cattle and horses. The Mexican government awarded him title to the island in 1829, mere months before he died. However, his family continued to live on the island, just not at Rancho Santa Cruz. Seven years after Father Ballí went on to his reward, the title he was granted was worth next to nothing because Texas declared independence from Mexico. The politics of the republic and the new government's inability to provide border security kept most people out of the Rio Grande Valley. All of that changed in 1845 when Texas joined the United States. One of the first acts of the U.S. government was to station troops in South Texas, many on Padre Island. Less than a year after Texas joined the union, fighting broke out at what is now Port Isabel. This initial conflict was followed by a series of skirmishes throughout the Rio Grande Valley. Prosaic places like Palo Alto, Matamoros, Reynosa, and Monterrey ran red with blood. While Samuel Colt's hammers were knocking out the southernmost border of the United States, a pair of castaways with a famous name had washed ashore on what was now being called Padre Island. In 1847 a man calling himself John Singer—he said he was the brother of the sewing machine magnate—and his wife, Johanna, were on a schooner that ran aground on Padre Island. Like many people they decided to stay on the island rather than risk trying to get back to civilization—it should be noted that attempting a land journey to a city from the southern point of Padre Island was a task of epic proportions. The roads were filled with bandits and Indians, the terrain was hostile and unforgiving, and the distances were seen as insurmountable. The Singers decided to build a house of driftwood at Rancho Santa Cruz, which was still occupied by Father Ballí's nephew Juan José Ballí. By all accounts John and Johanna Singer and Juan Ballí lived a

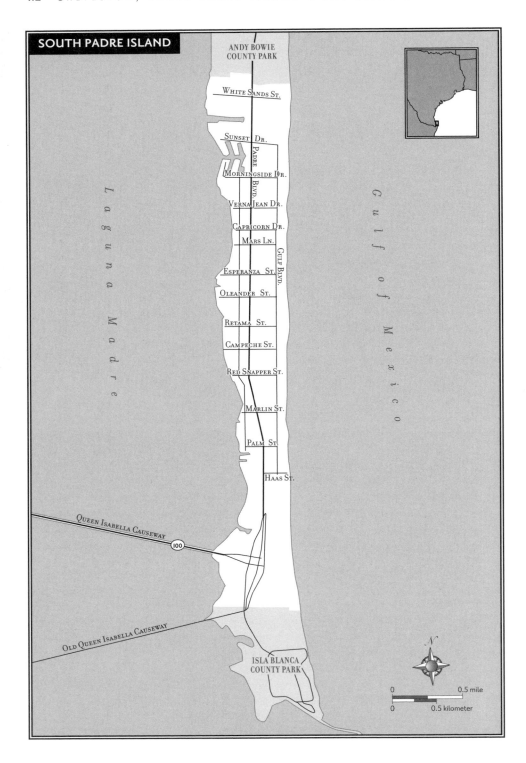

SOUTH PADRE ISLAND

ANDY BOWIE
COUNTY PARK

WHITE SANDS ST.

SUNSET DR.

PADRE BLVD.

MORNINGSIDE DR.

VERNA JEAN DR.

CAPRICORN DR.

MARS LN.

GULF BLVD.

ESPERANZA ST.

OLEANDER ST.

RETAMA ST.

CAMPECHE ST.

RED SNAPPER ST.

MARLIN ST.

PALM ST.

HAAS ST.

Laguna Madre

Gulf of Mexico

QUEEN ISABELLA CAUSEWAY

100

OLD QUEEN ISABELLA CAUSEWAY

ISLA BLANCA
COUNTY PARK

N

0   0.5 mile
0   0.5 kilometer

quiet life for the next six years, until the secession wind started blowing in the 1850s. By 1853 it had gotten so bad that Juan Ballí decided he had had enough of the gentleman farmer life and left. Eight years later when war broke out, the pro-Union Singers followed his lead and left, but not before burying what was estimated to be some $62,000 in coins and jewelry. The Civil War was far removed from Padre Island. But the Confederates did have troops stationed there, and the Union was blockading the coast to prevent guns and supplies getting to the front lines from Mexico. In May of 1865, a month after Lee surrendered, the last battle of the Civil War was fought at Palmito Hill in the Rio Grande Valley. The Confederates beat the Union soldiers in that battle.

Throughout the rest of the 19th century and into the beginning of the 20th, Padre Island could be summed up as simply a fishing camp for locals and celebrities. In fact, President Warren G. Harding referred to it as "my favorite little fishing spot at the end of the world." What drew notable

The Queen Isabella Causeway to South Padre Island.

figures like Harding were the rumors of mammoth fish and massive turtles. The fish were said to be as big as boats and the turtles the size of model Ts. Padre Island remained primarily a resort for sport fisherman up until the outbreak of World War II.

After Pearl Harbor the Army Air Forces established a base at what is today known as Cameron County Airport. The pilots used one of the most isolated parts of the island to practice bombing and strafing runs. Headlines from the time routinely warned residents and visitors not to swim in certain areas because they might be shot by diving aircraft. Aside from being a gunnery range for fighter pilots, Padre Island was used as a staging ground for some of the Coast Guard's anti-U-boat patrols during the war.

Life began to change drastically during the postwar years. In 1954 the Texas Department of Transportation completed the Queen Isabella Causeway, which established the first permanent connection between South Padre and the mainland. But perhaps the biggest change for Padre Island came in 1957 when the island was split in two. That was the year that Charlie Johnson, a former merchant mariner turned jack-of-all-trades turned ambitious real estate developer, and who just happened to be a cousin of Lyndon Johnson's, got the green light from the state of Texas to turn a condemned American Legion campground and fishing park on an area known as Redfish Bay into a port for boats caught in a storm on the Gulf of Mexico. The only problem was Redfish Bay wasn't on the Gulf, it was on the Intracoastal Waterway, separated from the Gulf by Padre Island.

This little logistical problem didn't bother Charlie Johnson at all. He just called up cousin Lyndon, who was then a U.S. senator, and had him do a little arm-twisting. And lo and behold, a channel was cut through the Padre Island National Seashore, which gave Charlie his port. Charlie Johnson was no idiot; he knew that getting a port built and maintaining it are two different things. Which is why he had his cousin in Washington do a little more arm-twisting to get the recently christened Port Mansfield declared a "Port of Refuge," which meant that the Army Corp of Engineers would be partially responsible for the upkeep. By 1962 Charlie Johnson was able to persuade the U.S. government to assume full responsibility for the channel, harbor, protective jetties, and navigational aides.

It so happened that 1962 was also the year that Padre Island National Seashore was scaled back; this opened hundreds of acres to public development for the first time in decades. Inevitably more and more visitors started trickling in, leading some people to think that Padre Island would rival Miami or Southern California as a tourist destination within ten years. That is until Hurricane Beulah came in 1966.

Beulah destroyed much of the small fishing village that was South Padre. Fortunately only a few hundred people were living there. The population remained very small throughout the rebuilding process and the next 12 years. In fact, in 1978 the entire year-round population of South Padre was barely over 300.

Not long after that spring break came. Almost every week in every March since the causeway opened, this about-as-far-south-as-you-can-go-and-still-be-in-the-U.S. spot on the map gets visited by almost one hundred thousand college kids who come with their six-packs, sombreros, string bikinis, and suntan lotion. When kids first made the annual pilgrimage to this land of fun in the sun, every college in Texas had spring break the same week; now they are staggered. What happened to change the release policy was essentially a riot in South Padre. In 1977 the college kids had set up a tent city and

Coastal defenses built prior to World War II.

virtual open-air drug bazaar along the beach—anything and everything was available. When the police eventually came to shut down this den of iniquity, things turned very nasty and violent. This led legislators to rethink the idea of allowing an army of college kids to overrun a small coastal town. Now Texas universities are supposed to stagger their spring breaks, although a majority of them still have spring break the second or third week of March. The other 11 months of the year, South Padre is still a small bedroom community with a population just under 2,500, although there is a slight increase during the winter months as elderly northerners migrate to the warmth of the Rio Grande Valley. Given the fact that South Padre's year-round population is only a fraction of the spring break crowd, it is no surprise that locals have mixed emotions regarding spring breakers. On the one hand they love the money the crowd brings, but on the other they hate what the crowd does. Living on South Padre during spring break has been likened to living on pre-Katrina Bourbon Street during Mardi Gras. However, it should be pointed out that if you go anytime other than March, you will basically have the place to yourself. You'll be hard-pressed to find people in bars or restaurants, almost every room in every hotel will be available, and you will be able to observe the wildlife in peace and quiet. The Rio Grande Valley has one of the most unusual ecosystems in the country; it is one of the few places in the U.S. where you will find wild, native parrots outside a K-Mart.

GETTING TO SOUTH PADRE

By Car
There is just one good way to get from Corpus Christi to South Padre by car, and that is via US 77. This long stretch of road runs straight through the King Ranch, one of the largest pieces of wilderness in the state. If you take this route, be sure you get gas and water before you leave Kingsville, and whatever you do, don't leave the highway, especially if you break down. Since the King Ranch is so big, fence riders are only in one section a week, and if you get lost it could take them quite a few days to find you. After you clear the King Ranch you will want to stay on 77 until you get to FM 100. Turn onto this road and it will take you straight to South Padre.

By Plane
If you are going to fly to South Padre, you'll probably want to fly into the Brownsville / South Padre Island Airport. In addition to saving you the drive, the airport offers free shuttle service to and from some hotels on the island, as well as easily accessible rental car agencies.

Car Rental
Be advised that while renting a car in Brownsville or on South Padre is a good idea, some agencies require that the car be returned to the location it was rented from, while others are more lenient.

Advantage Rent A Car: 956-982-1618; 700 S. Minnesota Ave, Brownsville, TX 78521

Avis Rent A Car: 956-541-9271; Brownsville / South Padre International Airport, 700 S. Minnesota Ave., Brownsville, TX 78521

Avis Rent A Car: 956-761-3183; 310 Padre Blvd., South Padre Island, TX 78597

Budget Rent A Car: 956-546-5119; 700 S. Minnesota Ave., Brownsville, TX 78521

Dollar Rent A Car: 956-982-2027; 700 S. Minnesota Ave., Brownsville, TX 78521

Enterprise Rent A Car: 956-574-9612; 700 S Minnesota Ave., Brownsville, TX 78521

Hertz Rent A Car: 956-542-7466; 700 S Minnesota Ave., Brownsville, TX 78521

By Bus or Train
Sadly, neither Greyhound nor Amtrak runs to South Padre. In fact, the nearest Greyhound stop to South Padre is in Brownsville, approximately 30 miles away. And unlike the Brownsville airport, Greyhound doesn't offer shuttle service to South Padre Island, which is why I strongly advise against trying to take the bus to South Padre.

By Boat
No cruise lines run to or from South Padre. However, if you want to sail your own boat here, the best place to dock it would be at the Anchor Marina Park just over the causeway in Port Isabel. They offer $10-a-night slip rentals, $25 if you want to use shore power. They also offer cheap monthly slip rates—$150 to $250, depending on the size of the boat and whether or not it has a/c. Their contact information is

One of the many ways to see the sights on the Texas coast.

Anchor Marina: 956-943-9323, (fax) 956-943-6638; www.anchormarinapark.com; E-mail: mark_anchor@hotmail.com; 40 Tarpon Ave., Port Isabel TX 78578

Getting Around South Padre

While South Padre is a large island, it is not that difficult to navigate. In fact, the entire populated area of South Padre Island is only 8 miles long and 1 mile wide at its widest point. Everything can be thought of as in relation to the main drag of Padre Boulevard. Everywhere on the island is either directly on this one road or just off it. If you decide to fly in and take advantage of the free shuttle from the airport to the hotel, don't worry about getting around once on the island. South Padre has an award-winning mass-transit system that is completely free. The Wave, South Padre's bus system, runs the length of the populated part of the island and into Port Isabel and back. The entire circuit of 28 stops takes about an hour and has stops approximately every three minutes. For more information call 956-761-1025.

LODGING

Hotels

Nowhere else in Texas is as dependent on seasonal tourism as South Padre. This fact means that every hotel changes its rates during the year. Some places may double or triple their room rates, depending on what is going on and what time of year it is. This means that research is extremely important; changing your hotel booking by a few days can save you up to three hundred dollars on the room.

COMFORT SUITES

956-772-9020
912 Padre Blvd., South Padre Island, TX 78597
Price: Moderate to Expensive
Credit Cards: AE, CB, D, DC, MC, V

The best thing about this hotel is that it offers discounts to the local Schlitterbahn water park as well as golf and dolphin-watching packages. It also has family suites that will comfortably hold six to eight people, with free high-speed Internet in every room, as well as fridges and microwaves. A pool, Jacuzzi, and free breakfasts are offered. A two-night minimum stay is required.

HOLIDAY INN SUNSPREE RESORT

956-761-5401
100 Padre Blvd., South Padre Island, TX 78597
Price: Inexpensive to Moderate
Credit Cards: AE, CB, D, DC, MC, V

This very nice Holiday Inn features two pools, lighted tennis courts, hot tub, gazebo, horseback riding, dolphin watching, whirlpool, two restaurants, an exercise room, and boatloads of other amenities, including my personal favorite, valet laundry. The building is six stories tall and has indoor corridors too. They do require a three-night minimum stay some seasons and impose a cancellation fee.

HOWARD JOHNSON INN-RESORT

956-761-5658
1709 Padre Blvd., South Padre Isalnd, TX 78597
Price: Inexpensive to Moderate
Credit Cards: AE, CB, D, DC, MC, V

This fairly bare-bones three-story, small-scale hotel has 91 units, all of which are off interior corridors. There is one two-bedroom suite and one three-bedroom suite, both of which come with kitchens. They also have a pool, whirlpool, and coin laundry and offer dual phone lines to each and every room, as well as voice-mail service. The staff is cheery and helpful.

LA COPA BEACH RESORT

956-761-6000
www.lacoparesort.com
350 Padre Blvd., South Padre Island, TX 78597
Price: Inexpensive to Expensive
Credit Cards: AE, D, MC, V

This hotel has a huge year-round price range, which means you have to be very well informed about the room you are booking. There are 146 units; 142 of them are one-bedroom, three are two-bedroom, and one is a three-bedroom. All are equipped with Internet access. The hotel has a beachfront pool, exercise room, whirlpool, coin laundry, and during the winter offers complimentary happy hour with their rooms. Weekly rates are available during certain parts of the year.

LA QUINTA INN AND SUITES

956-772-7000

7000 Padre Blvd., South Padre Island, TX 78597

Price: Inexpensive to Expensive

Credit Cards: AE, CB, D, DC, D, MC, V

This hotel has a $300 difference between low-end and high-end rooms year round. This is very strange, since all 147 rooms are one-bedroom. They do offer high-speed Internet, dual phone lines, voice mail, and safes in each room, as well as a beachfront pool, whirlpool, exercise room, and volleyball court.

QUALITY INN

956-761-4884

901 Padre Blvd., South Padre Island, TX 78597

Price: Inexpensive to Expensive

Credit Cards: AE, CB, D, DC, MC, V

This hotel has 49 one-bedroom units and, like many others on the island, definitely needs to be researched before you book a room. This is because the prices triple during peak times, and they require a two-night minimum stay. They do offer valet laundry service, dual phone lines, voice mail, high-speed Internet, safes, an outdoor pool, and a whirlpool.

RADISSON RESORT SOUTH PADRE ISLAND

956-761-6511

www.radisson.com/southpadretx

500 Padre Blvd., South Padre Island, TX 78597

Price: Expensive

Credit Cards: AE, CB, D, DC, MC, V

This 190-unit hotel is one of the best in South Padre. From the moment you drive up you know you are in the lap of luxury. Part of this is the location, on one of the most beautiful stetches of beach in the state of Texas, and the natural beauty is

only complemented by the hotel. With an opulent lobby, four lighted tennis courts, two pools, a whirlpool, a volleyball court, gift shop, in-room video games, valet laundry service, and a restaurant that serves fantastic food all day as well as cocktails in the evening and features live music on Saturdays, you could have a great vacation and never leave the hotel.

SHERATON BEACH HOTEL & CONDOMINIUMS

956-761-6551

www.sheraton.com/southpadreisland

310 Padre Blvd., South Padre Island, TX 78597

Price: Expensive

Credit Cards: AE, D, MC, V

With 256 units, this is the largest hotel on South Padre. Two hundred of the units are one-bedroom and 56 are two-bedroom, and all of them have private balconies looking over the beach. The hotel also has three pools, four tennis courts, a whirlpool, valet laundry service, gift shop, and in-room video games.

TRAVELODGE

956-761-4744

6200 Padre Blvd., South Padre Island, TX 78597

Price: Inexpensive to Expensive

Credit Cards: AE, D, DC, MC, V

This hotel is another one that triples its prices during peak times, so you need to research it before you book. They do have a pool and a sauna, all the rooms open on exterior corridors, and they don't require a minimum stay.

UPPER DECK HOTEL

956-761-5953

www.upperdeckhotel.com

120 E. Atoll St., South Padre Island, TX 78597

Price: Inexpensive to Moderate
Credit Cards: AE, D, MC, V

This is the only gay resort on South Padre. It is also the only hotel that is not open to children—all guests must be over 18. Down the street from the hotel is the local gay beach area. They also have a heated pool, patio, and hot tub area. Sadly, they don't offer much in the way of breakfast—a Danish, coffee, and juice. Strangely enough this hotel has some of the cheapest rates for spring break and Fourth of July. They also have rock-bottom winter prices. Since they are the only gay resort on the island, they also serve as a clearinghouse for GLBT information. If you want to know how to get to every gay bar in the Rio Grande Valley, what the major issues affecting the community are, or just where to get the new Scissor Sisters album, it's worth stopping in here. They are also the main sponsor for South Padre's twice-a-year Splash parties, an event the management claims they invented—and who's to say they didn't?

Condominiums

Staying at a condo on South Padre is not much different from staying at a condo anywhere else on the Texas coast: You need to book early, make sure that your reservation is intact before you leave, and walk the room with the manager before accepting possession of it. That being said, staying at the right condo might be a way to shave a few hundred off your housing expenses while you are down on the island.

Outside a hotel, front row, beachside.

GALLEON BAY CLUB

956-761-7808
4901 Laguna Blvd., South Padre Island, TX 78597
Price: Moderate to Expensive
Credit Cards: AE, D, MC, V

These quiet, out-of-the-way condos might be just what you are looking for if you don't want to stay directly on the main drag. The complex is a six-story building with 32 two-bedroom suites, all of which have kitchens. The management requires that all guests check in by 4 PM, because the office closes at five. They have one pool, a hot tub, and free on-site washer-dryer.

SEASCAPE CONDOMINIUMS

956-761-7166
117 E. Verna Jean Dr., South Padre Island, TX 78597
Price: Moderate to Expensive
Credit Cards: MC, V

This small condo complex, with eight two-bedroom suites with kitchens, has some of the strictest cancellation demands on the Texas coast. In addition to requiring a three-night minimum stay, they need 30 days' notice if you cancel, or they will assess a cancellation fee. The building is three stories and has no elevator. On the plus side, they do have free wash/dry service, a pool, and a whirlpool. They do offer weekly rates.

SUNCHASE IV CONDOMINIUMS BY SOUTH PADRE RESORT

956-761-6818
1000 Padre Blvd., South Padre Island, TX 78597
Price: Moderate to Expensive
Credit Cards: AE, MC, V

This place is big. I mean 14 stories big. I mean 72 units—10 one-bedroom, 50 two-bedroom, and 12 three-bedroom big. This

place has everything you need to be pampered: a sauna, a steam room, a whirlpool, four tennis courts, racquetball court, three pools, and an exercise room. They even offer weekly rates.

TIKI CONDOMINIUM HOTEL

956-761-2694
6608 Padre Blvd., South Padre Island, TX 78597
Price: Moderate to Expensive
Credit Cards: AE, CB, D, DC, MC, V

The first thing you notice about this condo is that it is nestled in a quiet corner of the beach. The moderately sized building houses 144 units—120 one-bedroom, 16 two-bedroom, and 8 three-bedroom suites, all with kitchens. It also has two pools, a sauna, a whirlpool, a coin-operated laundry, and requires a three-day cancellation notice.

Camping

South Padre is full of places to camp; from state parks to RV parks, this part of Texas has it all. The trick is determining what you will need to stay in each one.

ANDY BOWIE PARK

956-761-3704
7300 N. Padre Blvd., South Padre Island, TX 78597
Credit Cards: MC, V

This park on the northern edge of the town of South Padre features 18 spaces and is handicapped and wheelchair accessible. It also welcomes pets.

DESTINATION SOUTH PADRE RESORT / KOA

956-761-5665 or 1-800-TO-PADRE
www.destinationsouthpadre.com
1 Padre Blvd., South Padre Island, TX 78597

Some Texas beaches almost look like the New England coast, while other parts resemble Southern California.

This is the swankiest campground I have ever seen. They have incredible cabins, a heated 25-meter pool with lap lanes and a hot tub, a rec room with pool table and big-screen TV, and the list goes on and on. This must be the executive version of camping out.

ISLA BLANCA PARK
956-761-5494
www.spadre.com/parks
? Park Rd. 100, South Padre Island, TX 78597
Credit Cards: D, MC, V

This park is also one of the nicer campsites on the island. It has more than 800 spaces

available for both RV and tent camping, cable TV, an on-site restaurant, boat ramp, fishing pier, and laundry facilities. If you are bringing a motor home to South Padre, this should be one of the first places you consider staying.

RESTAURANTS
South Padre has an abundance of restaurants to choose from, the majority of them specializing in seafood. Due to space constraints I was only able to list a few.

B&A SEAFOOD MARKET
956-943-2461
604 Hwy. 100, Port Isabel, TX 78578
Credit Cards: AE, D, MC, V

Located just before you cross the causeway to South Padre Island, this market sells the freshest Gulf seafood and will ship anywhere in the U.S. They also have a good restaurant on site if you just can't wait to eat.

BLACKBEARD'S

956-761-2962
103 Saturn St., South Padre Island, TX 78597
Type of Food: Seafood
Price: Inexpensive to Moderate
Credit Cards: AE, D, MC, V

This is a good seafood place with a traditional menu. A standout is the blackened snapper Veracruzano, which is a lightly blackened snapper fillet smothered with sautéed onions, tomatoes, and green peppers, which the kitchen staff lovingly prepares.

DE LUNA

956-761-1920
201 W. Corral St., South Padre Island, TX 78597
Type of Food: Gourmet seafood
Price: Moderate to Expensive
Credit Cards: AE, D, MC, V

Chef Julio de Luna wanted this to be a unique experience in South Padre dining. He wanted to bring great food to the people at a price they can afford, and he wanted to do it without sacrificing on quality or alienating those who appreciate ultrafine dining. Amazingly enough he accomplished this. He did it by opening two restaurants under one roof. The downstairs menu is geared toward moderately priced but still innovative takes on the familiar classics of Gulf Coast fare. The upstairs is focused on innovative presentations in a thoroughly modern setting. This is definitely one of the gems of South Texas, and it would be a shame if you

Hard at work in a South Padre kitchen.

missed out on it. To ensure you get to eat here it is best to make a reservation.

DOLPHIN COVE OYSTER BAR

956-761-2850
Channel View Rd. inside Isla Blanca Park, South Padre Island, TX 78579
Type of Food: Seafood and burgers
Price: Inexpensive
Credit Cards: AE, D, MC, V

This open-air eatery is just as famous for dolphin watching as it is for its oysters and peel-and-eat shrimp. They also have daily specials. Tuesday and Thursday are 75-cent draft and $1.25 hot-dog days, while Wednesday and Friday are buy a half-dozen oysters and get the next half-dozen free. They have a large selection of burgers and three different types of tacos.

LAS OLAS

956-761-3767
340 Padre Blvd., South Padre Island, TX 78579
Type of Food: Gourmet
Price: Moderate to Expensive
Credit Cards: AE, D, MC, V

This beautiful, airy restaurant is located in the Peninsula Resort & Spa and is truly a gourmand's delight. They use only the best ingredients for dishes presented in the most artful ways. The restaurant is on an upper floor of the hotel, allowing diners an impressive view of all South Padre. Even better, they are open for breakfast, which means that there is finally a place on South Padre to get fantastic eggs Benedict at 11 AM. How things have changed!

LOUIE'S BACKYARD

956-761-6406
www.lbyspi.com
2305 Laguna Blvd., South Padre Island, TX 78597
Type of Food: Seafood
Credit Cards: AE, D, MC, V

Louie's is a venerable South Padre institution. It is where you can sit on the waterfront and watch glorious sunsets while a cool breeze blows in and the waiter brings out your perfectly cooked and seasoned mesquite-grilled snapper. The crab legs are also worth a try. The upstairs sports bar has an incredible number of TVs showing sporting events of all kinds, as well as darts, pool, and video golf. During spring break this is the hottest concert spot on the island, drawing national acts, thousands of college kids, and a cash-prize bikini contest that sends two winners on an all-expense-paid trip to Hawaii.

NATURALLY'S HEALTH FOOD STORE & CAFÉ

956-761-5332
1817 Padre Blvd., Suite 3, South Padre Island, TX 78579
Price: Inexpensive to Moderate
Credit Cards: AE, D, MC, V

This is proof positive that South Padre has come a long way: a good organic food restaurant. The food is excellent, and they aren't afraid to let you choose exactly how you want it prepared. It's nice to have a place that isn't afraid to serve granola, yogurt, or tofu.

PALM ST. PIER BAR & GRILL

956-772-7256, 956-772-7437
204 West Palm St., South Padre Island, TX 78579
Type of Food: Seafood
Price: Inexpensive
Credit Cards: AE, D, MC, V

The kitchen here is filled with fantastic shrimp cooks. In fact, they are so good they have won awards for it—first place three years running at the World Championship Shrimp Cook Off. The first year they won with their Captain Morgan Shrimp (sautéed in Captain Morgan sauce); the year after that they won with Honey Chipotle Shrimp (fried shrimp with dipping sauce and cold corn relish); and the year after that they won with Admiral Shrimp (sautéed in a sweet potato—jalapeño puree and served with cranberry relish and green beans—it makes my mouth water just to think about it). And if that is not enough, the kitchen also offers to cook whatever you catch and serve it with two sides.

PELICAN STATION

956-943-3344
www.pelicanstation.net
201 South Garcia St., Port Isabel, TX 78578
Type of Food: Seafood and steak

Price: Inexpensive
Credit Cards: AE, MC, V

Located in the terminal for the old Rio Grande Rail Road, this airy and well-lit diner-style eatery is one of the nicer family-oriented restaurants around South Padre. It is definitely worth stopping in for a bite and can offer a welcome respite from life on the island.

PIRATE'S LANDING

956-943-3663
www.pirateslandingrestaurant.com
110 North Garcia St., Port Isabel, TX 78578
Type of Food: Seafood
Price: Inexpensive to Moderate
Credit Cards: AE, MC, V

This pirate-themed seafood restaurant is right next to the most famous lighthouse in the state of Texas, one of the first sights you see when you pull into Port Isabel. It's the place with the big "WELCOME TO PORT ISABEL" sign just above the water. The food is good, and the setting truly makes an impression, especially after you've driven all the way from Corpus.

SALTY DOG'S CAFÉ

956-761-9550
1 Padre Blvd., South Padre Island, TX 78597
Type of Food: Breakfast
Price: Inexpensive
Credit Cards: AE, D, MC, V

This breakfast nook, which opens at 7:30 AM, is tucked away at the Sea Ranch Marina, which can make it hard to find. However, it is well worth the search for the best breakfast tacos on South Padre Island. They also serve great pancakes.

SCAMPI'S

956-761-1755
206 N. Aries St., South Padre Island, TX 78597

Type of Food: Seafood
Price: Inexpensive
Credit Cards: AE, CB, D, DC, MC, V

This restaurant is situated just right for viewing unforgettable sunsets, and to go with those memorable images is a menu that is just as unforgettable. Over the years the kitchen staff have proved themselves adept at handling the classics—oysters Rockefeller, calamari, and filet mignon—as well as producing some new twists, like Peanut Butter Shrimp, Lobster Filo Burrito, and Flounder Georgette, to name a few. This is definitely a place to take your appetite and your curiosity.

SEA RANCH RESTAURANT

956-761-1314
www.searanchtx.com
1 Padre Blvd., South Padre Island, TX 78597
Type of Food: Seafood and steak
Price: Inexpensive to Moderate
Credit Cards: AE, MC, V

This place is known for a little bit of a wait, the discomfort of which is quickly alleviated by the beauty of the marina and the glory of the food. The red snapper is famously good. However, the fried shrimp is an antihistamine dish—nothing to be sneezed at. But what really makes this place is all-around quality—even the food on the kids' menu is good. Oftentimes restaurants treat their younger patrons as an afterthought, and the food reflects this attitude. Fortunately, the Sea Ranch doesn't; they make sure that all the food they serve is excellent.

TEXAS MOON

956-761-3110
5800 Padre Blvd., South Padre Island, TX 78597
Type of Food: Burger joint and seafood
Price: Inexpensive
Credit Cards: AE, D, MC, V

This restaurant has one of the most pictur-esque names on the coast. The two words bring forth line after line of lyrical poetry, much the same way the kitchen here brings forth plate after plate of good burg-ers and sandwiches. In addition to the time-honored sandwich they also serve seafood and steaks, all of which are worth checking out.

YUMMIE'S BISTRO COFFEE SHACK
956-761-7526
www.spadre.com/yummies.htm
708 Padre Blvd. (Franke Plaza), South Padre Island, TX 78597

A garden in winter.

Type of Food: Breakfast
Price: Inexpensive
Credit Cards: AE, D, MC, V

This is one of the premiere spots for early risers. The store is filled with the aroma of fresh-baked pastries, coffee, sandwiches, and everything else you need to get going in the morning, and many things that may go straight to the hips. The cheesecake is incredible, the key lime pie even better. The staff is extremely friendly and helpful, and the management makes sure that all the ingredients are fresh and never frozen.

ZESTE GOURMET MARKET AND CAFÉ

956-761-5555
3508 Padre Blvd., South Padre Island, TX 78579

This is the best place in South Padre to meet all your "exotic food" needs. They sell an A-to-Z of world-cuisine ingredients. Things like udon noodles, tahini, wasabi, Hoisin sauce, risotto, and orzo are available here, and to make things even better, the in-store café uses all the things they sell.

NIGHTLIFE

With literally dozens of bars and night-clubs to choose from in South Padre, my liver would hate me if I tried to review each and every one of them. So I picked a dozen of my favorites.

Old wrecks are not uncommon sights off the Texas coast.

CHAOS

956-772-1922
1601 Padre Blvd., South Padre Island, TX
78597

This isn't really a bar or a nightclub in any normal sense of the word—it is six different clubs clustered around a concert stage. The mini-clubs have names like Hollywood Star Karaoke and Daddy O's sports bar, but the most descriptive name is Chaos. During spring break this place is known for foam parties, MTV-hosted events, and thousands of college kids trying to get into the Pimp Gallery, aka the VIP section.

CLUB X/S

956-761-1343
6300 Padre Blvd., South Padre Island, TX
78597

This hot dance club appeals to the beautiful people, the DJ blasts some of the best current club hits, and everyone brings all the moves and the clothes that they've been saving. By the end of the night you could swear you're in Miami or LA.

COCONUTS

956-761-4218
www.coconutsspi.com
2301 Laguna Blvd., South Padre Island, TX
78597

When this club opened in 1990 it was one of the island's first—if not *the* first—*palapa* bars, which is a bar with a thatched roof and open sides. Now almost 20 years later it has been recognized by the Travel Channel and 1obest.com as one of the best, if not the best, bars on the island. The praise is not without merit. Coconuts features live music almost every night, parasailing and wave-runner rental during the day, and their menu is heavy on Jamaican-style jerk chicken dishes.

CORAL REEF LOUNGE

956-761-1813
www.coralreeflounge.com
5401 Padre Blvd., South Padre Island, TX
78597

This is the premiere karaoke bar on South Padre, primarily because it's the only place you will find karaoke every night of the week. The friendly bar staff, drink specials, NASCAR, and Green Bay Packers games have made it a favorite for the locals over the years.

GULF COAST OYSTER BAR

956-761-7867
3409 Padre Blvd., South Padre Island, TX
78579

A favorite with the locals, this beer and seafood joint knows how to cook their oysters, as well as their jambalaya and steaks. The low-key atmosphere characterized by an amiable and friendly crowd brings people back again and again.

ISLAND OASIS

956-761-4695
2412 Padre Blvd., South Padre Island, TX
78579

This sports bar features live music, pool tables, darts, foosball, and serves food. They open at noon and close at 2 AM. It's a nice laid-back kind of place, perfect for getting out of the afternoon sun for a few hours or avoiding spring-break crowds.

KELLY'S IRISH PUB

956-761-7571
101 E Morningside Dr., South Padre Island, TX 78597

Since this is the only Irish-themed bar on South Padre, it is also the only place to get a black and tan, Irish car bomb, or a black and gold while listening to live music, shooting darts, and eating free popcorn.

A musician practices before a show at a South Padre pub.

QUARTERDECK CLUB

956-761-6511
500 Padre Blvd. (at the Radisson Resort),
South Padre Island, TX 78579

The main reason for going to this upscale
hotel bar is to see Pelican West. For the last
10 years this Greensburg, Pennsylvania,
band has been playing here, and they have
adapted their act to the unique requirements of being a house band at a resort.
They do live video karaoke on Tuesday,
where in addition to singing, audience
members get to play any instrument for
the song. Thursday is show nights; this is
what has made Pelican West's name.
Throughout the year they do four one-hour
floor shows that utilize props, costumes,
videos, trivia, and prizes. They also take
requests every night.

SOUTH PADRE ISLAND BREWING COMPANY

956-761-9585
3400 Padre Blvd., South Padre Island, TX
78597

This is the only bar in South Texas with its
own brewery, and the decor reflects it. The
place is filled with late 19th- and early
20th-century brewing memorabilia like
burlap barley sacks, copper kettles,
posters, and thick-walled bottles—not the
thin ones now in use. Drinking a beer here
is a history lesson in the art of the brew.
They also serve an incredible plate of ribs.

TEQUILA FROGS

956-761-7522
205 W. Palm St., South Padre Island, TX
78597

This is *the* spring break destination on South Padre. Every night during Texas Week it is one big party—bikini and boxer contests, bathing suits, body shots, and more. For some of these early twenty-somethings, this will be the last chance they get to experience life without inhibitions; in a few months they graduate and go on to the real world of the 9-to-5.

TOM & JERRY'S BEACH CLUB BAR & GRILL

956-761-8999
3212 Padre Blvd., South Padre Island, TX 78597

If it's playoff time, you want to be here. It doesn't matter what the sport is—football, basketball, baseball, or hockey—they have it on one of their many TVs, and if it's not, then the friendly and helpful staff will be glad to put it on. They also are the local headquarters for NTN trivia; in fact they do so well that they are usually ranked in the top two hundred sites in the country.

WANNA-WANNA BEACH BAR & GRILL

956-761-7677
5100 Gulf Blvd., South Padre Island, TX 78597

This beachside bar can be hard to find. The trick is to look for a thatched hut with a pirate flag. When you find it you'll be glad, and your reward will be cheap drinks, good food, an unprecedented view of the beach, and bar staff that will make you feel like an old friend.

ATTRACTIONS

BEACHCOMBERS MUSEUM

956-761-5231
www.islandtraders.biz/books
104 W. Pompano St., South Padre Island, TX 78597

Founded by local authors Steve Hathcock and Kay Lay, this coffee shop / ice cream parlor / bookstore / museum is filled with fascinating stories, pieces of information, as well as artifacts gathered over the years. Mr. Hathcock has been so gracious as to draw up a treasure map for anyone wanting to do a little beachcombing. He'll tell you where to go to find Spanish doubloons, mastodon teeth, Civil War buttons, and arrowheads. He'll also tell you that under state law any Spanish coins or treasure found belongs to the state of Texas.

COMMEMORATIVE AIR FORCE MUSEUM

956-541-8585
www.rgvwingcaf.com
955 S. Minnesota Ave., Brownsville, TX 78521

Home to the Rio Grande Valley Wing of the CAF, this museum has a fine selection of vintage aircraft, as well as artifacts and memorabilia documenting America's journey into the air that date from the 1920s. They also have special exhibits detailing the history of the Brownsville Airport and a memorial to fallen World War II veterans from the Brownsville area.

EDINBURG SCENIC WETLANDS & WORLD BIRDING CENTER

956-381-9922
www.worldbirdingcenter.com
E-mail: moliva@edinburgwbc.com
714 S. Raul Longoria Rd., Edinburg, Texas 78539

This beautiful piece of undeveloped natural habitat is the perfect place to observe some of the five hundred bird species of the Rio Grande Valley, such as the green kingfisher. This 7 1/2-inch-long bird is unique among kingfishers for its emerald green crest, wings, and back. The orange of the male's breast seems indicative of the festivity that characterizes life in the tropics.

GLADYS PORTER ZOO

956-546-7187
www.gpz.org
500 Ringold St., Brownsville, TX 78521

Even though this zoo has been around only since 1971, it has quickly become recognized as one of the nation's best. It houses more than 1,600 animals on 26 acres and offers many different educational programs for young and old alike. Two of the most popular exhibits are Macaw Canyon, a free-flight aviary and tropical America habitat, and the Small World children's area. The zoo is constantly expanding its collection, some of the latest additions being a Komodo dragon and four female Bengal tigers.

LAGUNA MADRE NATURE TRAIL

1-800-SO-PADRE
7355 Padre Blvd., South Padre Island, TX 78597

These two 4-mile-long boardwalks, each made from recycled material, weave their way through the saltwater marshes of the Laguna Madre. They start at the Warbler Rest Area just off the sand flats by the South Padre Island Convention Center and take travelers to a pair of blinds that allow stealthy observation of the local fauna.

MUSEUMS OF PORT ISABEL

956-943-7602
www.portisabelmuseums.com
317 E. Railroad Ave., Port Isabel, TX 78578

This is really a complex of three museums—the Point Isabel Lighthouse and Lighthouse Keeper's Cottage, the Treasures of the Gulf Museum, and the Port Isabel Museum. The lighthouse keeper's cottage is open free to the public and serves as the box office for all three. You can purchase tickets to any one of the attractions or all of them there.

MUSEUM OF SOUTH TEXAS HISTORY

956-383-6911
www.mosthistory.org
121 E. McIntyre St., Edinburg, TX 78541

Located in a charming town that is only a Texas hop, skip, and jump (about 70 miles) from South Padre, this fantastic museum is definitely one of the best in the region, if not the whole state. It takes visitors through the whole of South Texas history and does so in a most impressive way. The experience borders on mind-blowing.

PALO ALTO BATTLEFIELD

956-541-2785
7200 Paredes Line Rd., Brownsville, TX 78521

This is the only park in the nation that is dedicated to the U.S.-Mexican War. It features a video and exhibit explaining the war, a short walking trail, and a battlefield overlook and way to understand how a war that happened more than 160 years ago has continued to impact modern U.S. society.

SCHLITTERBAHN WATERPARK

956-772-SURF
90 Park Rd., Hwy. 100, South Padre Island, TX 78597

The southernmost water park in the state of Texas, this has acres and acres of family fun. With 15 different rides, including 4 water coasters, a giant sand castle, a restaurant, and a bar, you could spend all day here and never do the same thing twice.

SEA TURTLE INC.

956-761-1720; turtle hotline: 956-380-9677
www.seaturtleinc.com
6617 Padre Blvd., South Padre Island, TX 78597

The many public beach centers along the Texas coast are usually equipped with lifeguards and some small store.

Founded by Illa Loetscher, aka "the Turtle Lady," this organization is dedicated to rescuing and caring for sea turtles as well as educating the public about the endangered amphibians. Over the years Loetscher has become well-known throughout Texas as an outspoken advocate for these beautiful animals, and her organization is recognized as one of the best sea turtle research facilities in the country.

SOUTH PADRE ISLAND CENTER

956-943-0051
2 Wallace L. Reed Rd., South Padre Island, TX 78597

This former Coast Guard station, built in 1923, is the only historic building on South Padre Island. Its distinctive New England–style architecture and prominent lookout tower have made it a local land-

mark. It served as a functioning Coast Guard station until the late 1970s, when budget cuts and reorganization forced its closure. In 1987 the University of Texas at Brownsville / Texas Southernmost College renovated it and turned it into their first extension campus. It now houses the University's South Padre Island Technical Education Center and is a favored location for small meetings. They do offer tours to the public.

SOUTH PADRE ISLAND VISITOR CENTER SAND CASTLE

600 Padre Blvd., South Padre Island, TX 78597

This is the largest year-round sand castle in the state of Texas. It is built and maintained by Sons of the Beach Sand Castle Wizards, world-renowned sand castle

Busking on South Padre for a few extra bucks.

architects, who change the castle to reflect the seasons. This is a year-round treat for locals and tourists alike.

UNIVERSITY OF TEXAS PAN AMERICAN

956-761-2644
www.utpa.edu/csl
100 Marine Lab Dr., South Padre Island, TX 78597

Founded in 1973, this research lab is open to the public and displays various marine species native to the area and conducts research on things like the "Role of disturbance in determining community structure and development of vegetation of barrier islands," which deals with the human impact on the distribution of organisms in a barrier island ecosystem.

EVENTS

For a sleepy coastal town, South Padre has quite a bit going on. In fact, hardly a week goes by that there isn't something to do here. Whether it's the state surfing championship, a beauty pageant, or a film festival, South Padre makes sure that something is always going on. Please be advised that since date and locations change year to year and are very dependent on weather, it is best to call ahead.

January

SOUTH PADRE ISLAND POLAR BEAR CLUB NEW YEAR'S DAY DIP

January 1
1-800-SOPADRE

What better way to celebrate the New Year than to jump into the Gulf of Mexico at noon and follow that by eating black-eyed peas, which is a southern tradition, and drinking champagne?

LONGEST CAUSEWAY RUN & WELLNESS WALK
First Sunday in January
956-943-2262

This annual event sends runners and walkers down the length of the Queen Isabella Causeway. It also brings people from all over the country.

SPI MARKET DAYS
Third week of January
956-761-6746

An arts and crafts show that features many local and statewide artists.

WINTER TEXAN GOLF CLASSIC
Third weekend of January
1-800-SOPADRE

This senior golf tournament is open only to those over 55 years of age who are resident winter Texans and who don't play the South Padre Island Women's Golf Association. It is a chance to meet some new people who can show you how to shave a few strokes off the back nine. Remember, to play you have to register the week before the tournament.

TASTE OF THE ISLAND AND TRADE SHOW
Third Monday in January
956-761-4412

This is a foodie's dream. All the best restaurants on the island give away free samples of their signature dishes, and the biggest names in the food industry show off their latest products.

ALL YOU CAN EAT PANCAKES
Last Sunday in January
956-761-4412

Although this lasts only from 7:30 to 10 AM, it is distinctly possible that this event could take the cake for most pancakes served per hour in the entire state of Texas. They also serve orange juice, sausages, and bacon.

February

TAILS OF SPI KITE FESTIVAL
First weekend in February
956-761-1248

This free event is fun for the whole family; it shows off the constant winds of South Padre and is a celebration of kites.

FLAVOR OF LAGUNA MADRE
Second weekend in February
956-943-7602

This annual fund-raiser for the Port Isabel Historical Museum features a silent auction, the finest dishes, and the best wines, all for a tax-deductible donation.

SPICE: SOUTH PADRE ISLAND CHILI EXPO
Second Sunday in February
956-761-4412

This is the real deal, the biggest and baddest chili cook-off in South Texas. Chili chefs come from miles around to see who has the hottest, tastiest, most intense chili. Doors open to the public at noon, and if you go, be prepared to be amazed with recipes like "Buzzard's Breath Chili," where the chef hangs ripe jalapeños in a cheesecloth sack in the side of the pot to add the pure flavor without the spice.

WINTER TEXAN SNOWBIRD EXTRAVAGANZA

February 14–15
1-800-SOPADRE

Geared for the hundreds of senior citizens, this lifestyle expo features seminars on everything from Medicare to asset management, along with live music.

SOUTH PADRE ISLAND MARKET DAYS

Third Weekend in February
956-761-6746

This is another installment of the semi-regular arts and crafts show. It features local artists, artisans, jewelers, and crafts people.

ROTARY WINTER TEXAN FISH FRY

Third Sunday in February
1-800-SOPADRE

On the Texas coast you can chart the changing of the months by the foods being cooked. In the winter it's fish, in spring crawdads, in summer barbecue. This particular fish fry is held at the local Schlitterbahn water park and features live music.

ISLE-DITTER DOG

Third Sunday in February
956-943-3888

This is a celebration of all things canine. It involves an "old-fashioned dog race," canine costume contest, canine cakewalk, picture corner, and a silent auction, all to benefit the Laguna Madre Humane Society.

HERB EXTRAVAGANZA

February 25
956-748-3027

Thrown by the Cameron County Master Gardener Association, this annual event brings award-winning authors to speak about the finer points of gardening and features programs, exhibits, and demonstrations geared toward the neophyte, the old hand, and everyone in between. There's also a fresh herbal lunch.

MUSIC OF THE NIGHT

Last week in February
956-772-9097

This musical review is known for showcasing the body of work of a particular composer. In 2006 the featured artist was Andrew Lloyd Webber.

March

HEAT WAVE CAR SHOW

First week in March
512-252-0283

This touring show is a celebration of the automobile in modern urban America. It features hydraulic and audio competitions as well as live entertainment.

SPRING BREAK TUNER BASH & CAR SHOW

Second weekend in March

Whereas the focus of the Heat Wave show is on labors of love, the focus of this is on cars that are professionally customized, and primarily those that have professionally customized stereo systems. This is because the editors of *Super Street, Import Tuner, Turbo,* and *Car Audio & Electronics* are on hand to judge the vehicles.

TEXAS WEEK / SPRING BREAK

Second week in March
1-800-SO-PADRE

This is it, the big one. Students from all over the state of Texas converge on South Padre in the thousands for concerts and partying. This week brings some of the biggest names in the music industry to town.

April

SPI KID'S PEDAL-N-DASH DUATHLON
First Sunday in April
1-800-SO-PADRE

This is a three-stage race that is sure to work out the little ones. It starts with a beach run, then goes to a bike ride, and ends with another beach run. It is open to children of all ages.

SOUTH PADRE EASTER ISLAND EASTER EGG SCRAMBLE
Easter Sunday
1-800-SO-PADRE

This three-hour event is for children 12 and under and sends them running all over the back lawn of the visitor center looking for candy- and toy-filled eggs.

KIDS CUP OFFICIAL JUNIOR ANGLER FISHING TOURNAMENT
Third weekend in April
956-943-0011

This is one of the newer events on the South Padre calendar, and it is designed to introduce kids 10–16 to the world of tournament fishing. It begins with a mandatory dinner meeting in which the rules are laid out; the future fishermen hit the water the next day.

ANNUAL TEXAS STATE SURFING CHAMPIONSHIP
Third Sunday in April
www.tgsa.org

For Texas surfers this is the biggest event of the season. It's more for the bragging rights than the prize money. The fact that the winner of this competition gets to say that he or she is the best in Texas is a big deal, and it brings out the best in Texas. It should be noted that this event is held only if the surf is up.

SOUTH PADRE ISLAND SPLASH
Last weekend in April
956-761-5963
www.upperdeckhotel.com

This twice-a-year—one to start the summer and one to end it—gay pride party draws more than two thousand men, women, and transgenders to the island to have a blast. For some people it is the first time they feel accepted in the Rio Grande Valley; for others it is just another circuit party. Either way it's a good time. The organizers claim that this was the first Splash party in the U.S.

MISS INTERNATIONAL SOUTH PADRE ISLAND
Last weekend in April
956-207-4032

In the world of beauty pageants, this one is unique—a fairly small competition that allows international participants. Another unique aspect is that it doesn't require contestants to have gone through another pageant to qualify. In other words, it is open to everyone, regardless of their experience level.

May

MEMORIAL SURFING EXPRESSION SESSION
Early May
956-943-1562

All surfers are invited, no matter where they are from, although the prizes can only go to surfers from the Rio Grande Valley. The date of this event depends on the surf report.

SPI WINDSURF BLOWOUT
First weekend in May
1-800-SO-PADRE
www.spiwindsurfing.com

This annual windsurfing competition, held just north of the South Padre Island Convention Center, brings out some of the best in Texas. It is sponsored by the South Padre Island Windsurfing Association and the South Padre Island Convention and Visitor's Bureau.

PEDAL TO PADRE
First weekend in May
956-451-1500
www.riverrockets.com

This annual bike ride draws hundreds of Texas cyclists every year. It starts at the Brownsville Event Center, winds across the Queen Isabella Causeway, and ends at Louie's Backyard on South Padre, which makes it one of the most scenic rides in the state.

MEMORIAL WEEKEND VOLLEYBALL
Memorial Day weekend
956-761-2420

This is the biggest beach volleyball competition in South Texas, and it draws players from all over the state. It features men's, women's, and mixed doubles tournaments.

MEMORIAL DAY WEEKEND FIREWORKS ON THE BAY
Memorial Day weekend
1-800-SO-PADRE

South Padre summer weekends are known for one thing—fireworks—and this is the event that kicks them off. From Memorial Day until Labor Day, every Friday night fireworks are shot off on the bayside of the island between Marlin and Red Snapper Streets.

July

FOURTH OF JULY FIREWORKS OVER THE BAY
July 4
1-800-SO-PADRE

The annual Fourth of July fireworks extravaganza starts at sundown, lasts about an hour, and is launched at the same site as the regular fireworks displays.

ANNUAL BEACHCOMBERS ART SHOW & SALE
Last weekend in July
956-425-4994

This show draws artists from all over the southwestern United States, and despite the name, the pieces exhibited are not limited to things found on the beach.

August

TEXAS INTERNATIONAL FISHING TOURNAMENT
First week in August
956-943-TIFT
www.tift.org

This is the largest bay and deep-sea fishing tournament in the state. It involves the waters of both South Padre and Port Isabel and usually draws upward of 1,200 competitors.

LADIES KINGFISH TOURNAMENT
Second weekend in August
956-761-4412
www.spichamber.com

This is a more recent and much smaller fishing tournament. It has been around only for about 30 years and usually draws approximately 250 competitors. What it lacks in size it more than makes up for in social interaction. It is one of the few tournaments with an actual awards ceremony.

DUEL OF THE DUNES
Last weekend in August
956-451-1500
www.unlimitedsportsadventures.com

This is a relay triathlon-plus-mystery-events geared for life on the island. Events include running, paddling, biking, and more, and organizers accept only the first 100 teams. They also don't allow on-site registration.

September

SPI BEACH VOLLEYBALL / LABOR DAY TOURNAMENT
Labor Day weekend
956-761-2420

This tournament is a two-person team open with men's, women's, and mixed divisions. It also features cash prizes.

LABOR DAY FIREWORKS ON THE BAY
Labor Day
1-800-SO-PADRE

This event closes out the fireworks season on South Padre Island. It occurs on the bayside of the island between Marlin and Red Snapper streets at sundown.

RUFF RIDER REGATTA
Labor Day weekend
www.ruffrider.net

This annual catamaran race is one of the most beautiful events to watch. The boats running and tacking through the azure waters of the bay, the crews deftly maneuvering to try to steal the other boats' wind— ah, it truly is a sight to behold.

SPI FILM FESTIVAL
Third weekend in September
www.spifilmfestival.com

While this festival may not have the notoriety of Sundance or even South by South West, it does bring some really good movies.

WALK FOR WOMEN
September 29–October 1
956-761-4231
www.spiwalkforwomen.org

This fund-raiser consists of a banquet, silent and live auction, bay fishing tournament, barbecue, and awards ceremony, as well as the walk. The proceeds raised go to help local women who are struggling with breast cancer.

October

SOUTH PADRE ISLAND SPLASH
First weekend in October
956-761-5953
www.upperdeckhotel.com

The lineup for this three-day festival means little to people who are not in the world of drag queens and don't know what the phrase "trade bar" means. However, for those who are in the know, this is one of the biggest events in the country and certainly the biggest in the state. It brings over five thousand GLBTs to a tropical island for a beach party.

SOUTH PADRE ISLAND 1/2 MARATHON AND TRIATHLON
Columbus Day weekend
210-695-6430
www.rogersoler.com

This is a huge event. It has an individual half marathon, a four-person relay half marathon, an adult triathlon, and a kid's beach ball triathlon.

SPI BIKEFEST MOTORCYCLE CONVENTION & RALLY
Mid-October
www.spibikefest.com

Bikers from all across North America converge on South Padre for what is called "a roar by the shore." Participants get an armband, a souvenir pin, dog tags, and a ticket to the Saturday night concert at Schlitterbahn Waterpark and are entered to win a brand-new motorcycle.

PORT ISABEL'S LIGHTHOUSE MARKET DAYS
Second weekend in October
956-943-2262
www.portisabel.org

This arts and crafts fair at the famous Port Isabel lighthouse includes music, food, vendors, and sidewalk sales.

SAND CASTLE DAYS
October 19–22
1-800-SO-PADRE
www.sandcastledays.com

This weeklong festival brings some of the most talented artists in the world to compete in the Masters of Sand competition. These professional sand sculptors shape everything from fantasy castles to depictions of ancient myths. The competition also has an all-ages amateur class and offers sand castle lessons for "the masters of the future."

PORT ISABEL DÍA DE LOS MUERTOS (DAY OF THE DEAD) CELEBRATION
October 28
956-943-2262
www.portisabel.org

This traditional Mexican festival features cemetery tours, theater, dances, presentations, and lots of really cool skeletons and sugar skulls. If you have never been to a Día de los Muertos festival, it is definitely worth going to. They are always fun.

WOMEN'S TIP OF TEXAS GOLF CLASSIC
Last weekend in October
956-533-6114

Some of the local motorcycle crowd partakes of what South Padre is known for.

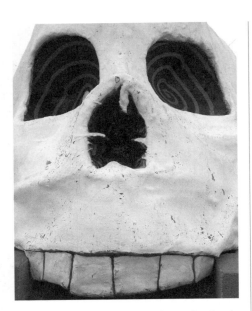

Skulls, especially sugar ones, are featured at Día de los Muertos, the traditional Mexican Day of the Dead holiday.

November

WORLD'S CHAMPIONSHIP SHRIMP COOK OFF

First Friday in November
956-943-2262
www.portisabel.org

Like almost any big-time cook-off, this one brings teams from all over to show just who has the best recipe. Some of these people have been working all year to perfect a new recipe. If you love shrimp, you need to be here.

TEXAS SENIOR OPEN

November 6–11

GALA SCHOLARSHIP FUNDRAISER AND AUCTION

November 18
956-761-4412

This is an annual benefit to help send students from South Padre to college.

SOUTH PADRE ISLAND DIVISION I INVITATIONAL BASKETBALL TOURNAMENT

November 24–25
1-800-SO-PADRE

This tournament brings some of the biggest teams in college basketball to South Padre for two days. In the past the tournament has hosted legendary teams like Auburn, Oklahoma State, Wisconsin, and Iowa State. If you like college sports, this is for you.

LIGHTING OF THE ISLAND

Last Saturday in November
1-800-SO-PADRE

New York and Washington, D.C., light trees for Christmas; in Texas we think that's not enough. So we bring Santa and Mrs. Claus down, sing some Christmas carols, and light up an entire island.

COMMUNITY CAROLING AT THE LIGHTHOUSE

Last Friday in November

This old-fashioned event brings choirs, brass bands, and members of the community together to sing at the Port Isabel Lighthouse.

December

HERE COMES SANTA WEEKEND

First weekend of December

This holiday celebration involves horseback riding with Santa, sand castle building with Santa, and dolphin watching with Santa. It also has some non-Santa-oriented events like the Island of Lights Parade, the Lighted Boat Parade, and the Bicycle Beach Bash. Local businesses get into the spirit of the season, too. Restaurants hold drawings for children's bicycles, and hotels/motels offer special rates.

ISLAND OF LIGHTS HOLIDAY PARADE

First Friday in December
956-761-2582

This annual parade has $3,000 in prize money to the top three entries in three categories, which makes the participants work that much harder on their floats. The event is also part of the "SPI Here Comes Santa Claus Weekend," which means that Santa Claus will be in attendance.

ANNUAL CHRISTMAS LIGHTED BOAT PARADE

First Saturday in December
956-943-2262

This celebration occurs up and down the Texas coast each year and is a variation of the "launching of the fleet" ceremony. The launching or blessing of the fleet is traditionally done in the spring at the beginning of the fishing season. This is sort of the bookend to that, in that it celebrates the end of the season and the safe return of the vessels.

NEW YEAR'S EVE FIREWORKS DISPLAY

December 31
1-800-SO-PADRE

The annual midnight fireworks display on the bay side of the island between Marlin and Red Snapper Streets.

SPORTS AND RECREATION

Golf

There is not an actual golf course on South Padre Island, but that shouldn't stop you from bringing your clubs. Ten minutes from South Padre in Laguna Vista is a beautiful 18-hole course, and if you are willing to drive 30 minutes to Brownsville there are three clubs, two of which have two different courses.

In late November the Port Isabel Lighthouse is the site of community caroling.

BROWNSVILLE GOLF CENTER

956-541-2582
1800 W. San Marcelo Blvd., Brownsville, TX 78526

This public 18-hole, 6,144-yard par 70 has moderately priced green fees, and the course, restaurant, and lounge have all been renovated. Quite a few berms have been added to the front nine to make things more interesting.

RANCHO VIEJO RESORT

956-350-4000 or 1-800-531-7400
www.playrancho.com
1 Rancho Viejo Dr., Rancho Viejo, TX 78575

Located just outside Brownsville, this destination golf resort has two par-70 courses with the most poetic course names I've ever seen. The first is the Diablo Course, which is 6,847 yards, and the second is the Angel Course, which is 6,301 yards. Both courses live up to their names and make this definitely a fun place to play. There is also a full-service hotel with a pool, restaurant, bar, and all the amenities you would need for a weekend getaway.

SOUTH PADRE ISLAND GOLF CLUB

956-943-5678
www.spigolf.com
1 Golf House Rd., Laguna Vista, TX 78578

This top-of-the-line 18-hole, par-72 course is just across the causeway from South Padre. It features rolling hills and rough that is really rough—don't be surprised if your lost ball spooks some local wildlife.

VALLEY INTERNATIONAL COUNTRY CLUB

956-546-5331, 956-548-9199 (tee times)
95 Country Club Rd., Brownsville, TX 78520

This is one of the only courses in the valley to offer both an 18-hole and a 9-hole course. The 18 is a beautiful, 6,538-yard par 70, while the 9 is a none-too-shabby 1,000-yard par 3. They also have tennis courts, a wellness center, and a good restaurant that serves lunch and dinner.

SHOPPING AND SERVICES

FOX BEACHWEAR

956-772-041
1200 Padre Blvd., South Padre Island, TX 78597

This is one of the best places to get all those trinkets and things that seem so essential at the moment—shot glasses, T-shirts with slogans about being drunk, a Texas flag bikini, a sarong, a sombrero, a henna tattoo, and a plastic necklace. If they sold beer this would be a one-stop shop for spring break necessities.

ISLAND EQUESTRIAN CENTER

956-761-4677
www.horseonthebeach.com
South Padre Island, TX 78597

Seeing the beach from horseback is a fun and unique way to experience South Padre. The main problem always has been that the time you spend with the horse is too short. Fortunately Island Equestrian Center rents them by the day as well as the hour, and they have plenty of mounts to choose from. They do require reservations and offer group rates.

ISLANDS

956-761-6919
2500 Padre Blvd., South Padre Island, TX 78579

Don't expect to find T-shirts with double entendres here; this store specializes in men's and women's upscale designer-name clothing in tropical styles and breezy colors. If you are looking for something that radiates confidence and success but is still practical and loose, go no further.

JIM'S BEACH RENTALS
956-761-2130

This business has no fixed address; it's just somebody renting folding chairs and umbrellas. Which may seem shady, but if you plan on spending an extended period in the sun, canvas-and-oak deck chairs and a large umbrella may seem like a worthwhile expense.

SANDPIPER RESORT WEAR AND GIFTS
956-772-1055
310 Padre Blvd. (inside the Sheraton Hotel), South Padre Island, TX 78597

This store specializes in upscale beach-wear, with brands like Tommy Bahama, Luau, Maui Jim, and Island Slipper. It is the place to go for that stylish, laid-back tropical look.

SHIP SHAPE
956-762-2111
5212 Padre Blvd., South Padre Island, TX 78597

This store can be a bit pricey, since it offers clothes and accessories geared for the older, more-established visitor. You can find conservative-yet-still-fun clothes for a day at or near the beach, and it even carries binoculars for the eco-tourists.

SHIP SHAPE TOO
956-761-6550
1 Padre Blvd., South Padre Island, TX 78597

This midrange jewelry store is owned by the same people who own Ship Shape. It is located in the lobby of the Sea Ranch Restaurant and features fairly unusual pieces that are worth a look. They tend to lean more toward the amber side of the spectrum, but they do stock diamonds.

Tattoos have become a spring break tradition.

SONNY'S BEACH SERVICES
956-761-5556
www.spadre.com/sonnys.htm
E-mail: vlgfegsbs@aol.com
100 Padre Blvd. (inside Holiday Inn Sunspree)
310 Padre Blvd (inside Sheraton)
500 Padre Blvd (inside Radisson)
South Padre Island, TX 78597

These guys are the original beach-rental agency. They do it all: parasailing, wave runners, electric cars, dolphin watching, sunset cruises, deep-sea fishing, banana-boat rides—and they stock beach essentials (clothing, towels, chairs, umbrellas). If you need anything while you are at South Padre, they can get it for you, and if you want to do anything, they can make it happen.

SOUTH PADRE ISLAND KITEBOARDING

956-772-1098
www.southpadrekiteboarding.com
5208 B Padre Blvd., South Padre Island, TX
78597

This is the only shop/school dedicated solely to kiteboarding. If you want to try out this fun new sport, they are the best people to talk to. Their lessons even include wave-runner support, which may not seem like much until you are a good mile and a half from where you started and you can't get the kite airborne to pull you back.

SOUTH PADRE SURF COMPANY

956-772-7272

This is a surfing school and board rental agency. If you have ever dreamed of shredding the waves, then this is your first stop. Their motto is "We'll get you on your feet," which is no small task, considering that even paddling out can be problematic. But have no fear: Owners Gene and Rachel will help you to do it all correctly, including showing you how to make it to where the good waves are. You can even get a clear digital picture of you catching your first wave, and a nice safe, soft board so you don't get hurt if you wipe out.

WINDCHASERS

956-761-7028
www.kiteshop.com
102 E Swordfish St., South Padre Island,
TX 78597

This is an essential store for kiteboarders and kite enthusiasts. The prices are competitive, and the staff is knowledgeable. If you need to get spare gear, want to know how kiteboarding got started, or how a box kite flies, this is the place to go.

WOODY & DICK'S BEACH SHACK

956-772-1955
Beach Access Road 2
South Padre Island, TX 78597

This store sells everything you need for a day at the beach, from ice and coolers to sunscreen and swimwear. They also sell food—primarily of the ballpark variety, like hot dogs and nachos. If you forgot something or see something on the beach that you wish you had, this is the place to get it.

Historical houses and other attractions can have unpredictable opening hours, so always check ahead before visiting.

4

Information
Essential Details

The main thing that people who come to visit Texas don't understand is the weather. As Dan Rather famously pointed out, "While the rest of the nation has four seasons, Texas has three. They are summer, almost summer, and not summer." This is especially true with the Texas coast, where summer weather usually lasts seven to eight months, with high humidity being a constant. In fact, it is not uncommon to see temperatures soaring as early as late April. I know of weeks where the 9 AM temperature was 85 degrees with 80 percent humidity. The temperature climbs another 10 degrees in four hours, and it doesn't cool off until well past 9 PM. This keeps most people indoors during the summer months.

What to Wear / What to Bring

However, if you are determined to be outside during the heat, there are steps you can take to minimize the amount of damage the sun will do to you. Be sure to bring lots of cotton shirts, because the dangers posed by the sun and the heat cannot be overstressed. Walking down the street during a Texas summer can be described as trying to claw your way through a warm, wet, wool blanket. Shorts are a good idea any time of the year—when it is 70 degrees in December, long pants are almost unnecessary. And finally, you need a good hat. As a train-hopping friend of mine told me, "You don't realize how much a hat cuts the sun until you don't got one." You will also need at least an SPF 35 sunscreen. The Texas sun can be brutal, and because of the relative humidity and high pollution levels here, it is not like other Sunbelt states, such as Florida. Very few people tan in Texas; most just burn.

Water
Always drink plenty of water. Since the heat index can easily reach 100°F and still maintain 80 percent humidity, dehydration is a common occurrence in this part of Texas. The best answer is to drink at least 20 ounces of water every hour. This is primarily because just standing outside, you will be sweating.

Outdoor Activity
Any physical activity during the heat of the day, which usually lasts until about 6 PM in the summer months, is generally regarded as insane. This is because of the high probability of suffering from heat cramps, heat exhaustion, and in the worst cases, heatstroke. No matter what you are doing, if you are feeling faint or lightheaded, stop and find a cool place to sit down.

Extreme Heat: Symptoms and Treatment

Heatstroke, heat exhaustion, and heat cramps are forms of hyperthermia, each with accompanying physical symptoms. The primary causes of these ailments are extreme heat, high humidity, vigorous exercise under the sun, and dehydration. The populations most at risk are infants, the elderly, athletes, or outdoor workers.

HEAT CRAMPS

The mildest form of hyperthermia, this generally affects people who sweat a lot. The sweating expels the necessary salts and electrolytes from the body, which may lead to cramps in the abdomen, arms, and legs. To treat heat cramps, sit in a cool shady spot, drink clear juice, water, or a sports beverage, and do not return to strenuous activity for two to three hours after the cramps have subsided. This is because further physical activity may lead to heat exhaustion or heatstroke. Seek medical attention if you have heart problems, are on a low-sodium diet, or the cramps persist for over an hour.

HEAT EXHAUSTION

A mild form of hyperthermia, symptoms include heavy sweating, paleness, exhaustion, nausea, vomiting, fatigue, weakness, headache, muscle cramps, dizziness, feeling lightheaded, and fainting. The pulse rate will be fast and weak, breathing fast and shallow. Seek medical attention if the symptoms are severe, last longer than an hour, or if the person has heart problems or high blood pressure. To treat heat exhaustion, move victims to a cool, shady, or air-conditioned environment, have them rest, and give them cool, nonalcoholic beverages.

HEATSTROKE OR SUNSTROKE

The symptoms of heatstroke (also known as sunstroke), may mimic those of a heart attack, and different people exhibit different symptoms; however, some of the most common are high body temperature, lack of sweating, rapid pulse, shortness of breath, hallucinations, confusion, agitation, disorientation, seizures, coma, and finally death. If not treated immediately, victims of heatstroke may suffer permanent organ damage. To treat victims of heatstroke: Notify emergency services and then begin to cool victim. Move the victim to a shady spot or air-conditioned environment, apply cool water to the skin, fan to promote sweating, place icepacks or cold wet rags under armpits and groin, monitor body temperature with thermometer, and continue cooling efforts until body temperature drops below 103.

The best way to avoid heat-related illness and injury is to stay hydrated (principally with water and sports drinks), avoid vigorous physical activity outdoors, wear light-colored loose-fitting clothes, and take frequent breaks to rest and hydrate. (*From the U.S. Centers for Disease Control*)

HURRICANES

Like the rest of the Gulf Coast, Texas has hurricanes, tropical storms, and tropical depressions. From June to November everyone watches the weather to see how long it will be before they get hit. Even if it is just a tropical storm, in the Gulf people start stockpiling the necessities—food, water, gas, candles, lamp oil, ammunition, bandages, cigarettes to barter with. People know that there is no pattern to hurricanes; big storms can come as early as June or as late as November. They can flatten cities or peter out harmlessly. If a hurricane is headed their way, people routinely cover their windows with plywood and move everything inside. They know staying put or evacuating is a gamble. If you stay put you may wind up injured or worse. You might watch a neighborhood get flattened—have no phone, gas, electric, or water service for days, possibly weeks. People know that if they are going to evacuate, they have to know every possible route and leave early and drive far; otherwise they might be stuck on the freeway for 16 hours or more with no food, no water, dwindling gas, and with a hurricane still barreling down on them.

If you are here when a storm is approaching, be sure to check the National Hurricane Center's Web site, www.nhc.org, for the most up-to-date information, and the local media's Web sites for survival kits.

MOSQUITOES

These pesky little bugs are a constant problem on the Gulf Coast, especially at night. If you plan on being out after dark, the best thing to do is to bring mosquito repellent with you everywhere you go; if you don't, be prepared to spend hours swatting. As far as I can tell, there is no best mosquito repellent; the creams get sweated off too quickly, and the sprays smell. The best bet, in my experience, is to use Off Skintastic about once every three hours.

HAZARDS IN THE GULF OF MEXICO

Jack-up rigs are ever-present in this part of the Gulf. If going offshore, be sure to steer clear of them.

Jellyfish and Portuguese Man-of-Wars

These beautiful and harmless-looking creatures can pack a serious sting. They pose no life-threatening danger, unless you are severely allergic. However, it should be noted that even washed up dead on the shore, they can still hurt you. The best way to treat a jellyfish or a Portuguese man-of-war sting is to douse the infected area with rubbing alcohol to clean it and with meat tenderizer to neutralize the poison. Then wrap it with a clean, wet rag. If you get stung, don't go back in the water, as the salt will only make it hurt worse. You also should expect a minor amount of swelling. If the pain and any swelling don't subside after approximately 72 hours, seek medical help.

Catfish/Hardheads

These fish are not particularly dangerous unless they are caught. This is because they won't spine you unless you attempt to

Trying to catch a breeze.

hold them. If you are spined by a saltwater catfish, or, as they are lovingly called here, a hardhead, douse the puncture with rubbing alcohol and bandage it. That's about all that can be done. Expect some minor swelling; if this persists longer than a week, you should probably see a doctor.

Sharks

Because of the usually high water temperature, shark attacks are a rare occurrence on the Texas coast. However, sharks have been known to come as close as a quarter-mile to shore. The only thing that can be advised here is to stay close to shore.

MEDICAL EMERGENCIES

Texas has some of the finest doctors in the world. Every city and county has a fully functional 911 service, and the capabilities of an EMT are surprisingly high. That being said, the necessary contact information for the major hospitals along the Texas coast follows.

Galveston

University of Texas Medical Branch: 409-772-1011; 301 University Blvd #604, Galveston, TX 77555

Shriners Hospital for Children (burns hospital): 409-770-6600; 815 Market St., Galveston, TX 77550

Corpus Christi

Christus Spohn Health System–Memorial: 361-902-4000; 2606 Hospital Blvd., Corpus Christi, TX 78405

Christus Spohn Heath System–Shoreline: 361-881-3000; 600 Elizabeth St., Corpus Christi, TX 78404

Kindred Hospital Corpus Christi: 361-986-1600; 6226 Saratoga Blvd., Corpus Christi, TX 78414

South Padre Island

Valley Baptist Medical Center / South Padre Island Family Practice Center: 956-772-1911; 3401 Padre Blvd., South Padre Island, TX 78597

The Bishop's Palace in Galveston is one attraction not to be missed.

5

If Time Is Short

This is the part of the book for those who may be in town for only a night or two, or have a harried schedule while they are in town.

GALVESTON

Best Hotel

SAN LUIS HOTEL
409-744-1500 or 1-800-445-0090
www.sanluisresort.com
5222 Seawall Blvd., Galveston, TX 77551
Price: Expensive
Credit Cards: AE, D, MC, V

Best Restaurant

BISTRO LECROY
409-762-4200
2021 Strand, Galveston, TX 77550
Type of Food: Louisiana/Creole
Price: Moderate to Expensive
Credit Cards: AE, D, MC, V

Best Bar

MOLLY'S IRISH PUB
409-763-4466
2013 Postoffice St., Galveston TX 77550
Price: Inexpensive to Moderate
Credit Cards: AE, D, MC, V

Best Live Music

THE OLD QUARTER ACOUSTIC CAFÉ
409-762-9199, 409-737-4915
413 20th St., Galveston, TX 77550

Price: Inexpensive to Moderate
Credit Cards: AE, D, MC, V

Best Attractions

FOR NATURE LOVERS

ANAHUAC NATIONAL WILDLIFE REFUGE
409-267-3337
509 Washington Ave., Anahuac, TX 77514

FOR SIGHTSEERS

THE BISHOP'S PALACE
409-762-2475
1402 Broadway, Galveston, TX 77550

FOR KIDS

SCHLITTERBAHN WATERPARK
409-770-9283
www.schlitterbahn.com
2026 Lockheed Dr., Galveston, TX 77551
Price: Moderate to Expensive
Credit Cards: AE, D, MC, V

FOR ADULTS

STRAND THEATRE
409-763-4591
www.strandtheatregalveston.org
2317 Mechanic St., Galveston, TX 77550

CORPUS CHRISTI

Best Hotel

OMNI HOTELS
361-887-1600
www.omnihotels.com
900 N. Shoreline Blvd., Corpus Christi, TX
78401
Price: Moderate to High
Credit Cards: AE, CB, D, DC, MC, V

Best Restaurant

KATZ 21 STEAK & SPIRITS
361-884-1815
www.katz21.com
317 Mesquite St. (at the corner of
Lawrence), Corpus Christi, TX 78401
Type of Food: Steak and seafood
CC: AE, D, MC, V

Best Bar

MARTINI BAR
361-814-2010
6601 Everhart Rd., Suite D-5, Corpus
Christi, TX 78413
Credit Cards: AE, D, MC, V

Best Live Music

HOUSE OF ROCK
361-882-7625
ww.texashouseofrock.com
511 Star St., Corpus Christi, TX 78401
Credit Cards: AE, D, MC, V

Best Attractions

FOR NATURE LOVERS

TEXAS STATE AQUARIUM
361-881-1200/800-477-GULF (4853)
www.texasstateaquarium.org
2710 N. Shoreline Blvd., Corpus Christi
Beach, TX 78402

FOR SIGHTSEERS

CENTENNIAL HOUSE
361-882-8691
411 N. Upper Broadway, Corpus Christi, TX
78401

FOR KIDS

COLE PARK
361-561-0253
1526 Ocean Dr., Corpus Christi, TX 78404

**CORPUS CHRISTI MUSEUM OF
SCIENCE AND HISTORY**
361-826-4667
www.ccmuseum.com
1900 N. Chaparral St., Corpus Christi, TX
78401

FOR SPORTS FANS

**CORPUS CHRISTI HOOKS (AA AFFILI-
ATE OF THE HOUSTON ASTROS)**
361-561-4665
www.cchooks.com
734 E. Port Ave., Corpus Christi, TX 78401

FOR ADULTS

**CORPUS CHRISTI SYMPHONY
ORCHESTRA**
361-883-6683 or 1-877-286-6683
www.ccsymphony.org
555 N. Carancahua St., Corpus Christi, TX
78401

SOUTH PADRE

Best Hotel

**RADISSON RESORT SOUTH PADRE
ISLAND**
956-761-6511
www.radisson.com/southpadretx
500 Padre Blvd., South Padre Island, TX
78597
Price: Expensive
Credit Cards: AE, CB, D, DC, MC, V

Best Restaurant

DE LUNA
956-761-1920
201 W. Corral St., South Padre Island, TX
78579
Type of Food: Gourmet seafood
Price: Moderate to Expensive
Credit Cards: AE, D, MC, V

Best Bar

SOUTH PADRE ISLAND BREWING COMPANY
956-761-9585
3400 Padre Blvd., South Padre Island, TX
78597
Credit Cards: AE, D, MC, V

Best Live Music

LOUIE'S BACKYARD
956-761-6406
2305 Laguna Dr., South Padre Island, TX
78597
www.lbyspi.com
Credit Cards: AE, D, MC, V

Best Attractions

FOR NATURE LOVERS

EDINBURG SCENIC WETLANDS & WORLD BIRDING CENTER
956-381-9922
www.worldbirdingcenter.com
E-mail: moliva@edinburgwbc.com
714 S. Raul Longoria Rd., Edinburg, TX
78539

FOR ADULTS

BEACHCOMBERS MUSEUM
956-761-5231
www.islandtraders.biz/books
104 W. Pompano St., South Padre Island,
TX 78597

A "state of the art" laundromat.

FOR KIDS

SEA TURTLE INC.
956-761-1720; turtle hotline: 956-380-9677
www.seaturtleinc.com
6617 Padre Blvd., South Padre Island, TX
78597

TOURIST INFORMATION

All cities mentioned here, whether they are major ones like Galveston and Corpus or minor ones like Rockport and Palacios, have city councils or a chamber of commerce that helps to promote the city. They can almost all be contacted via e-mail links on their Web sites.

Galveston

Galveston Chamber of Commerce: 409-763-5326; www.galvestonchamber.com; 519 25th St., Galveston, TX 77550

Galveston Island Convention and Visitors Bureau: 409-797-5100; www.galveston.com; 2106 Seawall Blvd., Galveston, TX 77550

Galveston Historical Foundation: Strand Visitors Center: 409-765-7834; 502 20th St., Galveston, TX 77550

Clear Lake, Kemah, Seabrook

Clear Lake Area: 281-488-7676; www.clearlakearea.com; 1201 W. NASA Road 1, Webster, TX 77598

Angleton

Greater Angleton Chamber of Commerce: 979-849-6443; www.angletonchamber.org; 445 E. Mulberry St., Angleton, TX 77515

Texas City

Texas City–La Marque Chamber of Commerce: 409-935-1408; www.texascitychamber .com; 9702 Emmet F. Lowry Expressway, Texas City, TX 77591

Freeport

Freeport Visitors & Park Office: 979-233-3306; 500 N. Brazosport Blvd., Freeport, TX 77541

Lake Jackson

Brazosport Chamber of Commerce: 979-265-2505; www.brazosport.org; 300 Abner Jackson Pkwy., Lake Jackson, TX 77566

Palacios

Palacios Chamber of Commerce: 361-972-2615; www.palacioschamber.com; 420 Main St., Palacios, TX 77465

Port Lavaca

Port Lavaca–Calhoun County Chamber of Commerce: 361-552-2959; www.portlavaca info.com; 2300 State Hwy. 35 North, Port Lavaca, TX 77979

Corpus Christi

Corpus Christi Visitors Bureau & Chamber of Commerce: 361-881-1800 or 1-800-678-6232; www.corpuschristi-tx-cvb.org; 1201 N. Shoreline Blvd., Corpus Christi, TX 78401

Visitor Information Centers: Downtown at Interstate 37; 1-800-766-2322; 1823 N. Chaparral St., Corpus Christi, TX 78401

Labonte Park at Nueces Bay: 361-241-1461; 1433 I-37, Corpus Christi, TX 78410

South Padre Island

South Padre Island Convention & Visitors Bureau: 956-761-3000; www.so padre.com; 7355 Padre Blvd., South Padre Island TX 78597

Town of South Padre Island Convention & Visitors Bureau: 956-761-6433; www.sopadre.com; 600 Padre Blvd #A, South Padre Island, TX 78597

One of the South Padre public visitor centers.

Brownsville

Brownsville Convention & Visitors Bureau: 956-546-3721 or 1-800-626-2639; www.brownsville.org; P.O. Box 4697, Brownsville, TX 78523

Brownsville Chamber of Commerce: 956-542-4341; www.brownsvillechamber.com; 1600 University Blvd., Brownsville, TX 78520

BIBLIOGRAPHY

As J. Frank Dobie wrote in the *WPA Guide to Texas* in 1939, "Almost contemporary with the discovery of Texas by Europeans was the beginning of its literature." It may seem strange to some that books on Texas predate the existence of the state of Texas by three hundred years. However, you have to remember that for centuries, going to Texas and surviving the trip was considered a feat worth writing about. The first book to discuss Texas was Cabeza de Vaca's travel narrative, *La Relación de Cabeza de Vaca*, in which he describes being held captive by Indians and making his escape. A full copy of this amazing travel narrative can be found online at www.library.txstate.edu/swwc/cdv/index.html. The version at this site is a very good translation of the 1555 edition, although it should be noted that the first edition was published eight years earlier with 42 more words in the title. For the next 450 years books were continually published about Texas. The incredible span of time involved in Texas literature, plus the vast amount of books published in that time, helps to explain why there are more books about Texas than almost all the other states combined. In fact, there are so many that booksellers created a category specifically for them: Texana. To try to list all of them would require a book of no less than 700 pages. So I picked some of my favorites that are still in print, an act that will inevitably upset some. There are many more available at university libraries and rare bookstores.

Barthelme, Donald. *Snow White*. New York: Simon & Schuster, 1965 (187 pp., $12.00). It may seem odd that this imaginative reworking of the classic fairy tale by one of the late-20th century's premiere postmodern writers would have anything to do with Texas. Shows how little you know. Barthelme grew up in Houston. He was the director of the Houston Contemporary Arts Museum, helped found the University of Houston Creative Writing Program (one of the first in the nation), and lived in Houston most of his life. His writings may not directly reflect Houston, but they still should be read as a way to understand Houston.

Bickerstaff, Steve. *Lines in the Sand: Congressional Redistricting in Texas and the Downfall of Tom Delay*. Austin: University of Texas Press, 2007. (472 pp., $34.95). This much-needed book details the downfall of the most powerful man in Texas politics in a readable manner. The author is a UT law professor and former special assistant attorney general.

Bradfield, Bill, and Clare Bradfield. *Muleshoe & More*. Houston: Gulf Publishing Co., 1999 (218 pp. $15.95). This helpful dictionary/encyclopedia will help keep you from mangling some of the more difficult and unusual place names in Texas. It is also filled with the interesting bits of trivia that make a long car ride a little bit more enjoyable.

Borders, Gary B. *A Hanging in Nacogdoches: Murder, Race, Politics and Polemics in Texas's Oldest Town, 1870–1916*. Austin: University of Texas Press, 2006 (239 pp.). This book is important, not because it tells the story of James Buchanan, a black man who was sentenced to death for a crime he didn't commit. Hundreds of those cases happened and are still happening throughout the South and elsewhere. No, it is important because it describes why those cases happen. It gets into the power politics behind racism, shows how national trends can manifest themselves at the lowest levels, and how the personal rivalries of two people can lead to the death of a third.

Brands, H. W. *Lone Star Nation: The Epic Story of the Battle for Texas Independence*. New York: Random House, 2005 (582 pp., $16.95). This is perhaps the most recent and best book on the Texas war for independence, primarily because it spends as much time on the Mexicans as it does on the Texans. The author, a UT history professor, has a novelist's grasp of pacing and character. This moves into the realm of what Stephen Ambrose describes as "historians writing for a popular audience." Personally I think it a good thing because it means that he knows how to tell a story.

Byrd, Sigman. *Sig Byrd's Houston*. New York: Viking Press, 1955 (250 pp.). This is the best book ever written about Houston. The author was a reporter for the now-defunct *Houston Post* back in the forties and fifties. He worked the metro beat, writing about the city and its people—the musicians, junkies, sailors, cantina owners, prostitutes, and blacksmiths (yes, Houston still had blacksmiths operating in 1954). His writing was beautiful, his eye fantastic. He was the best newspaperman Houston ever produced, and this book should be read by everyone who lives, visits, drives through, or even hears about Houston. It should be passed out at the airport, placed next to the Gideon Bibles in the city's hotels, and kept in every home. It is that good.

Campbell, Randolph B. *Gone to Texas: A History of the Lone Star State*. New York, Oxford: Oxford University Press, 2003 (500 pp., $35.00). This historical overview takes readers from the arrival of the first humans up to the beginning of the Cold War. It keeps the myths pretty much intact. The heroes stay heroes, and the villains stay villains, and it never lingers long enough to get boring or uncomfortable.

Clayton, Lawrence, and Joe W. Specht, eds. *The Roots of Texas Music*. College Station: Texas A&M University Press, 2003 (235 pp., $19.95). This book runs the gamut—with chapters on jazz, country, blues, zydeco, classical, gospel, and Chicano, Czech, and Polish contributions—all of which are written by recognized authorities on the subject. It is a very interesting read and should be sold along with every musical instrument in the state of Texas.

Cohen, Rebecca S. *Art Guide Texas: Museums, Art Centers, Alternative Spaces, and Nonprofit Galleries*. Austin: University of Texas Press, 2004 (464 pp., $24.95). This guide is noble in its attempt and ambition, but sadly limited in its coverage. It favors the big established venues and not the fringe galleries where the really interesting stuff is going on or the public art spaces. This is a good introduction, but it is no way complete. Hopefully an expanded edition will be coming soon.

Davis, Steven L. *Texas Literary Outlaws: Six Writers in the Sixties and Beyond*. Fort Worth, TX: TCU Press. 2004 (511 pp., $35.00). This huge, rollicking, riotous book deals with the lives of the six writers who changed the very notion of what Texas is. Bud Shrake, Larry L. King, Billy Lee Brammer, Gary Cartwright, Dan Jenkins, and Peter Gent—their names may not be household words, but their writings are. They helped found *Texas Monthly* and wrote things like *Best Little Whorehouse in Texas* and *North Dallas Forty*. They redefined what it meant to be a writer in Texas, partied with Willie Nelson, and forged a literary community while doing it.

Dobie, J. Frank. *Tales of Old Time Texas*. Austin: University of Texas Press, 1928. This collection of folktales is by one of the greatest Texas writers of the early 20th century. Dobie's style is indicative of that period, as is the typography in the book and the illustrations.

When UT Press reissued it in 2000, they slapped a new jacket on it and left the interior remarkably unchanged, which allows today's reader to be able to see the pen-and-ink drawings next to the old-style typeface.

Federal Writers' Project. *Texas: A Guide to the Lone Star State*. Austin: Texas Monthly Press, 1986. Originally published New York: Hastings House, 1940, in the American Guide Series (718 pp.). This very useful and interesting guide can't stay in print. It was a project of the WPA and employed hundreds of local Texas authors through the Depression. After the Depression and World War II the publication lapsed. Then for the state of Texas's sesqui-centennial, Texas Monthly Press picked up the copyright, and now that edition has gone out of print too, although copies of it can still be found in libraries and on the Internet.

Fehrenbach, T. R. *Lone Star: A History of Texas and the Texans*. Cambridge, MA: Da Capo Press, 2000 (767 pp., $34.95). When it first came out, this phone-book-size history was fairly groundbreaking in the field of Texas history, as it was one of the first histories to focus less on the traditional heroes and more on the experience of what it was like to live during those times. Almost 40 years later this idea hasn't really caught on in Texas history classes. The idea of the hero on the white horse leading the charge still dominates the discussion; this book should be more widely read.

Light reading.

Gallaway, B. P., ed. *Texas: Dark Corner of the Confederacy*. Lincoln: University of Nebraska Press, 1994 (286 pp., $16.95). Drawn from a wealth of primary sources, this fascinating collection paints a beautifully grim picture of the day-to-day life of the lower classes in what was essentially a frontier territory far removed from the antebellum South. People seem to think that all over the South there were plantations and Scarlett O'Haras. That certainly wasn't the case in Texas, where in many places people still lived in log cabins. Sadly, the author doesn't spend enough time on Galveston—I have no clue how he can ignore the complete and total descent of a city into abject chaos.

Gilb, Dagoberto, ed. *Hecho en Tejas: An Anthology of Texas-Mexican Literature*. Albuquerque: University of New Mexico Press, 2006 (521 pp., $29.95). This celebration/collection/introduction to Texas Hispanic writers covers everything from prose to poetry to song. It is arranged historically and starts with Cabeza de Vaca and goes from there. While there are some things that are left out, like Coronado, this book paints a rich picture of the struggles Latinos have faced in the Lone Star State. It is definitely worth the read.

Greene, A. C. *The Fifty Best Texas Books*. Denton: University of North Texas Press, 1998 (92 pp., $21.95). This notorious collection of criticism started out as a magazine column in 1981, and it grew from there. It became famous as a guidebook to Texas literature and then infamous as a symbol of everything wrong with Texas literature. The original publication even prompted Pulitzer Prize winner Larry McMurtry to write the now famous essay, "Ever a Bridegroom: Reflections on the Failure of Texas Literature," in part to disprove the notion that there are 50 good Texas books.

Greer, James Kimmins. *Texas Ranger: Jack Hays in the Frontier Southwest*. College Station: Texas A&M University Press, 1993. Adapted from *Colonel Jack Hays: Texas Frontier Leader and California Builder*. New York: E. P. Dutton, 1952 (237 pp., $19.99). This entertaining biography of one of the more colorful characters of the Texas Republic is worth the read, even if it omits Hays's life after he left Texas.

Handbook of Texas Music. Austin: Texas State Historical Association, 2003 (391 pp., $24.95). This encyclopedic reference book of Texas musicians leaves out the Texas contribution to hip-hop. It would be much nicer if it had CDs and more entries.

Hilton, Conrad. *Be My Guest*. New York: Prentice Hall, 1957 (288 pp.). This biography about the man who founded Hilton hotels is incredibly mesmerizing. To think that Hilton hotels started in Texas—who would have guessed?

Landscapes of Texas. College Station: Texas A&M University Press, 1980 (158 pp.). This fantastic coffee-table book is a collection of pictures from *Texas Highways* magazine and is filled with gorgeous landscapes that make you understand exactly why people in Texas are filled with so much pride. It is amazing to see that these places exist and can look as pretty as they do.

La Vere, David. *Life among the Texas Indians: The WPA Narratives*. College Station: Texas A&M University Press, 1998 (270 pp., $19.95). This incredible book was culled from thousands of interviews conducted by WPA-employed historians in 1937 and 1938. It details life among the Caddo, Comanche, Kiowa, Lipan Apache, Tonkawa, and Wichita tribes. It gets into the social structures of the tribes, the relations between the tribes, and the relations of the tribes with Europeans. It should be noted that these interviews were conducted at a time when there were still people alive who had fought for and against U.S. expansion into the West. The Indians interviewed could still remember what life was like on the open range, and they tell the cowboy and Indian story a little differently.

Larson, Erik. *Isaac's Storm*. New York: Random House, 1999 (323 pp., $14.00). This incredible book tells how the great 1900 Galveston hurricane disaster happened. It details the failures that made it possible and the epic struggles of those who survived. This is a must-read.

Maril, Robert Lee. *Patrolling Chaos: The U.S. Border Patrol in Deep South Texas*. Lubbock: Texas Tech University Press, 2006 ($24.95). This digs deep into the closed society of immigration enforcement, and then it keeps going. It also digs deep into the dark heart of one of America's greatest problems and the peculiar psychology of border patrol agents.

The book was based on two years of field work. The author followed 12 Border Patrol agents, men and women, on their 10-hour shifts.

McComb, David G. *Galveston: A History*. Austin: University of Texas Press, 1986 (293 pp., $19.95). A very readable, if somewhat dry, history of the island that avoids embellishment and provides a good introductory overview to what life was like.

McMurtry, Larry. *Lonesome Dove*. New York: Simon & Schuster, 1985. What can be said about this novel that hasn't been said before? There is a reason why it won a Pulitzer. What can be said about the writer that hasn't been said before? There is a reason why he's a legend. If you want to understand the romance of the Texas West, you should read this book.

Minutaglio, Bill. *City on Fire: The Explosion That Devastated a Texas Town and Ignited a Historic Legal Battle*. New York: HarperCollins, 2003 (286 pp., $13.95). This is the best book about the Texas City explosion and fire. Minutaglio deals with the complicated issues of the recovery effort and subsequent lawsuit without losing any of his readers. The brilliance of his writing is in his Tom Clancy-ish pacing.

Powell, William Dylan. *Houston Then and Now*. San Diego, CA: Thunder Bay Press, 2003 (144 pp., $14.98). This beautiful coffee-table book is easily one of the most visually interesting books about Houston. It simply shows older pictures of Houston contrasted with the same places today. It helps drive home how fast the city reinvents itself.

Renaud, Jorge Antonio. *Behind the Walls: A Guide for Family and Friends of Texas Inmates*. Denton: University of North Texas Press, 2000 (218 pp., $14.95). Written by a three-time felon who is serving time for armed robbery, this long hard look at the Texas prison system does an admirable job of dealing with one of today's touchiest subjects. The author has a bachelor's degree in sociology, so he is trained to observe; he was also the editor of the Texas prison system newspaper.

Siegel, Stanley E. *A History of Texas to 1865*. Boston: American Press, 1981 (260 pp.). This well-written, very enjoyable book is one of the definitive ones on 19th-century Texas history. Sadly, it also is out of print.

A Political History of the Texas Republic: 1836–1845. Austin: University of Texas Press, 1956 (281 pp.). This is the book for the true Texas history buff. It deals with all the intrigue and backroom deals that helped create the short-lived republic. It is especially interesting to read about U.S. troops slipping across the border to meet up with Sam Houston's retreating army, the feud between Mirabeau Lamar and Sam Houston, and the Texas Navy's involvement in the Yucatán rebellion.

Spellman, Paul N. *Spindletop Boom Days*. College Station: Texas A&M University Press, 2001 (266 pp., $29.95). This is the real deal—the first-person accounts of what life was like after the largest oil strike of the early 20th century. After the Lucas oil well blew and gave the world the iconic image of the gushing oil derrick, cities all over Texas became overnight boomtowns and had to contend with the problems that came with that, not the least of which were the fires, fistfights, roughnecks, and roustabouts. Spindletop was producing 70,000 barrels a day, an unheard-of number at the time. These boom years helped shape the world's perception of Texas as a place full of rich, backward people.

Tyler, Ron, and Lawrence R. Murphy. *The Slave Narratives of Texas*. Austin, TX: Encino Press, 1974 (143 pp.). This is a heartbreaking book. Collected from WPA interviews of former slaves and descendants of slaves, this book paints a vivid picture of just what man is capable of doing to another man. It should be read by every schoolchild, because it helps to destroy the notion that slavery was more humane in Texas.

Waters, Michael R. et al. *Lone Star Stalag*. College Station: Texas A&M University Press, 2004 (288 pp., $19.95). This is a well researched, in-depth look into the day-to-day life at what was the largest POW camp in the U.S. Waters and his team cover everything from the mundane to the tragic and in doing so illuminate one of the last untold stories of American involvement in World War II.

Wiggins, Melanie. *Torpedoes in the Gulf: Galveston and the U-Boats, 1942–43*. College Station: Texas A&M University Press, 1995 (280 pp., $15.95). Providing one of the most detailed accounts of a little-known but very important aspect of World War II, Wiggins helps to show how unrestricted submarine warfare in what many considered to be the U.S.'s backyard changed the way we felt about the war and ourselves.

Williams, Docia Schultz. *Ghosts along the Texas Coast*. Lanham, MD: Republic of Texas Press, 1993 (234 pp., $16.95). The title pretty well sums it up; this is a ghost tour in book form. The author helped bring ghost tours to San Antonio. The writing is sure to delight fans of the supernatural.

General Index

Woody & Dick's Beach Shack, 144
World's Championship Shrimp Cook Off, 140
World War I, 30
World War II, 11, 31
 outbreak of, 113

Y
Yaga's Cafe and Bar, 51
Yamato Japanese Seafood Sushi & Steakhouse
 (Galveston), 48

Yardam Restaurant (Corpus Christi), 82
yellow fever, 25
 outbreak of, 27
 return of, 29
Yummie's Bistro Coffee Shack (South Padre Island),
 126–27

Z
Zeste Gourmet Market and Café, 127
zoos, 91–92, 131

Lodging by Price

Inexpensive: under $75
Moderate: $75 to $100
Expensive: $100 to $150
Very Expensive: $150 and up

Corpus Christi
Inexpensive
  Bayfront Inn, 73
  Clarion Hotel, 74
  Fairfield Inn, 75
  Hawthorn Suites, 75
  Knights Inn-By the Beach, 75
  Quality Inn, 75–76
Inexpensive to Moderate
  Best Western Marina Grand, 73
Moderate
  Bahia Mar, 73
  Christy Estates Suites, 74
  George Blucher House Bed & Breakfast, 76
  Holiday Inn Emerald Beach, 75
  Island House Condominiums, 77
  Surfside Condominium Apartments, 77
  Villa La Casta, 76
Moderate to Expensive
  El Constante Condominiums, 77
  Fortuna Bay Bed and Breakfast, 76
  Gulfstream Condominiums, 77
  Ocean House, 76
  Omni Hotels, 75

Galveston
Moderate
  Bayou Shores RV Resort, 40–41
  Dellanera RV Park, 41
  Galveston Island Hilton Resort, 35
  Holiday Inn on the Beach, 35
Moderate to Expensive
  Avenue O Bed and Breakfast, 36–37
  Garden Inn, 38

  Inn at 1816 Post Office, 38
  Moody Gardens Hotel, 35
  Queen Anne Bed and Breakfast, 39
  Tremont House, 36
  Villa Bed & Breakfast, 39
Expensive
  Hotel Galvez, 35
  Island Jewel Bed & Breakfast, 38–39
  San Luis Hotel, 35–36
Expensive to Very Expensive
  Coastal Dreams Bed & Breakfast, 37–38
  Coppersmith Inn Bed & Breakfast, 38
  Grace Manor Bed & Breakfast, 38
  Lone Palm Bed and Breakfast, 39
  A Victorian Bed & Breakfast Inn, 39

Palacios
Inexpensive to Moderate
  Luther Hotel, 65

South Padre Island
Inexpensive to Moderate
  Holiday Inn Sunspree Resort, 118
  Howard Johnson Inn-Resort, 118
  Upper Deck Hotel, 119–20
Inexpensive to Expensive
  La Copa Beach Resort, 118
  La Quinta Inn and Suites, 119
  Quality Inn, 119
  Travelodge, 119
Moderate to Expensive
  Comfort Suites, 118
  Galleon Bay Club, 121
  Seascape Condominiums, 121
  Sunchase IV Condominiums by South Padre Resort, 121
  Tiki Condominium Hotel, 121
Expensive
  Radisson Resort South Padre Island, 119
  Sheraton Beach Hotel & Condominiums, 119

Dining by Price

Inexpensive:	under $25
Moderate:	$25 to $50
Expensive:	$50 to $75
Very Expensive:	$75 and up

Corpus Christi

Inexpensive to Moderate
Ancient Mariner Seafood Restaurant, 78
Bamboo Garden Chinese Restaurant, 78–79
Blackbeard's on the Beach, 79
Black Diamond Oyster Bar, 79
City Diner and Oyster Bar, 79
Mao Tai's Chinese Restaurant, 80
Origami Japanese Cuisine, 80
Pier 99, 80–81
Q Pub, 81
Tajmahal Indian Restaurant, 81
Water Street Market, 81–82
Yardam Restaurant, 82

Moderate
Jezebelle's Restaurant, 79

Expensive to Very Expensive
Katz 21 Steak and Spirits, 79–80
Republic of Texas Bar & Grill, 81

Galveston

Inexpensive
Fullen's Waterfall, 42
La Estacion, 44
Mario's Seawall Italian Restaurant, 44–45
Papa's Gourmet Pizza and Subs, 46
PHO 20, 46
Phoenix Bakery & Coffee Shop, 46
Queen's Barbeque, 46–47
Shrimp N' Stuff, 47–48
The Spot, 48
Sunflower Bakery, 48

Inexpensive to Moderate
Apache Mexican Cuisine, 41
Benno's on the Beach, 41–42
Juju's Hangout Bar, 44
Mosquito Caf_, 45
Olympia Grill, 45

Moderate
Saltwater Grill, 47

Moderate to Expensive
Bistro Lecroy, 42
Clary's Seafood Restaurant, 42
Luigi's Ristorante Italiano, 44
Rainforest Café, 47
Rudy & Paco's, 47
Yamato Japanese Seafood Sushi & Steakhouse, 48

Expensive
Gaido's Famous Seafood Restaurant, 42, 44
Palms M&M, 45

South Padre Island

Inexpensive
Dolphin Cove Oyster Bar, 123–24
Palm St. Pier Bar & Grill, 124
Pelican Station, 124–25
Salty Dog's Caf_, 125
Scampi's, 125
Texas Moon, 125–26
Yummie's Bistro Coffee Shack, 126–27

Inexpensive to Moderate
Blackbeard's, 123
Naturally's Health Food Store & Café, 124
Pirate's Landing, 125
Sea Ranch Restaurant, 125

Moderate to Expensive
De Luna, 123
Las Olas, 124